QUALITATIVE RESEARCH IN THE TIME OF COVID

NEW DIRECTIONS FOR THEORIZING IN QUALITATIVE INQUIRY

A BOOK SERIES EDITED BY NORMAN K. DENZIN AND JAMES SALVO

New Directions for Theorizing in Qualitative Inquiry consists of thematic edited volumes that help us understand the philosophical concepts undergirding theory and how to put theory into practice to bring about social justice. The chapters in each volume, from established and emerging scholars and largely drawn from papers at the annual International Congress of Qualitative Inquiry, represent new directions for incorporating theory into justice-oriented qualitative research. Taking particular interest in theorists who haven't yet had mainstream influence, the series is designed to reach a wide audience of scholars and students in the humanities and social sciences, including those seasoned in the philosophical language of theory and novices to theoretically-oriented research. The series aims to bring about experimental ways of reading lives to implement radical social change.

Books in the Series:

New Directions In Theorizing Qualitative Research: The Arts (2020)
New Directions In Theorizing Qualitative Research: Indigenous Research (2020)
New Directions In Theorizing Qualitative Research: Performance as Resistance (2021)
New Directions In Theorizing Qualitative Research: Theory as Resistance (2021)
Qualitative Research in the Time of COVID: Lessons Learned and Opportunities Presented During a Pandemic (2023)
Culturally Relevant Storytelling in Qualitative Research: Diversity, Equity, and Inclusion Examined through a Research Lens (2023)
Educational Media and Technology: New Developments in Remote Teaching, Machine Learning, Artificial Intelligence and Other Topics (2024)
Education and Sustainability: Applying the United Nations' 17 Sustainable Development Goals to Teaching and Learning (2024)

If you have a manuscript or a proposal for a book-length work, please send it to Norman Denzin (n-denzin@illinois.edu) or James Salvo (salvo3000@gmail.com). All books published by MEP are peer reviewed. We will acknowledge receipt of your material but it may be 4-6 weeks before we can provide initial feedback about your proposal.

QUALITATIVE RESEARCH IN THE TIME OF COVID

Lessons Learned and Opportunities Presented During a Pandemic

EDITED BY NORMAN K. DENZIN

AND JAMES SALVO

Gorham, Maine

Published by Myers Education Press, LLC
P.O. Box 424
Gorham, ME 04038

Myers Education Press is an academic publisher specializing in books, e-books and digital content in the field of education. All of our books are subjected to a rigorous peer review process and produced in compliance with the standards of the Council on Library and Information Resources.

Library of Congress Cataloging-in-Publication Data available from Library of Congress.

13-digit ISBN 978-1-9755-0521-9 (paperback)
13-digit ISBN 978-1-9755-0522-6 (library networkable e-edition)
13-digit ISBN 978-1-9755-0523-3 (consumer e-edition)

Printed in the United States of America.

All first editions printed on acid-free paper that meets the American National Standards Institute Z39-48 standard.

Cover design by Teresa Lagrange Design Service from Portland, ME.

Contents

List of Figures and Tables *vii*

INTRO Remembrance and an Ethics of Care: Living After the Event of the Pandemic's Coming into Being 1
James Salvo

ONE Teaching and Learning of Qualitative Research in Times of COVID-19 in Mexico 7
Edith J. Cisneros-Cohernour, Roger J. González-González, and Karla E. Atoche-Rodríguez

TWO "They Could Count on Me": Educational Leadership Educators' Development of a Culture of Caring During the COVID-19 Pandemic 23
Jill Channing and Georgina E. Wilson

THREE Viral Epistolary: A Digital Community for Individual and Collective Writing at the Time of the First COVID-19 Wave 41
Ciro De Vincenzo, Anita Franceschi, and Monica Massari

FOUR LMK, Blue-Heart Emoji & Smiling Face: Using SMS Pedagogy Amid the COVID-19 Pandemic 55
Ezequiel Korin

FIVE COVID-19 Lockdown: An Arts-Based Narrative 75
Aravindhan Natarajan

SIX Finishing a Dissertation in Lockdown: "I Might Not Live to Become an Academic" 99

Carol Rogers-Shaw

SEVEN Reflections on Cross-Cultural Feminist Research During COVID: Guiding Principles, Challenges Faced, and Lessons Learned 117

Cathy Raymond

EIGHT Refugee Youth Amidst Multiple Pandemics: Mobilizing Hope and Solidarity through Collective Memory Writing 133

Emina Bužinkić

About the Authors *149*

Index *153*

List of Figures and Tables

Figure 3.1:	Workflow to write, receive, and reply to a letter.	44
Figure 5.1:	The Cleveland Orchestra, Severance Hall.	76
Figure 5.2:	Cellist, the Cleveland Orchestra.	76
Figure 5.3:	Staying Put at Home.	78
Figure 5.4:	Taking in Small Changes in the Garden.	79
Figure 5.5:	Hostas in the Garden.	79
Figure 5.6:	The Sunroom Couch.	80
Figure 5.7:	Appreciating the Mundane.	80
Figure 5.8:	George Floyd.	82
Figure 5.9:	United States Capitol under Attack on January 6, 2021 (Based on *Washington Post* Footage).	82
Figure 5.10:	Venturing Out to Nature Center.	83
Figure 5.11:	The Garage Quartet.	84
Figure 5.12:	Listening to a Quartet in the Garage.	84
Figure 5.13:	Enjoying Live Music after a Long Time.	84
Figure 5.14:	Man Walking Dog.	85
Figure 5.15:	Man without Mask.	85
Figure 5.16:	Camping to Socialize.	86
Figure 5.17:	Setting Up Tent in the Garage.	86
Figure 5.18:	Camping in the Garage.	87
Figure 5.19:	Natalie Goldberg Remembers John Lewis (Zoom class).	88
Figure 5.20:	Natalie Goldberg's Writing Class on Zoom.	88
Figure 5.21:	Virtual Graduation Ceremony.	89

Figure 5.22: Waiting in Line to Get Vaccinated. 90

Figure 5.23: Volunteers at the Vaccination Site. 90

Figure 5.24: Mother Excited about Child Getting Vaccinated. 91

Figure 5.25: Vaccinated against COVID-19. 91

Figure 5.26: Registered Nurse Prepares the COVID-19 Vaccine Shot. 92

Figure 5.27: Volunteer Disinfecting Chair. 92

Figure 5.28: Thanks to Essential Workers, Volunteers, and Medical Personnel Working at the Vaccination Site. 93

Figure 5.29: Spring Is Here. 94

Figure 5.30: There Is Hope. 95

Figure 5.31: Neighbor Walking Dog. 95

Figure 5.32: Neighbor Working on Car. 96

Figure 5.33: Graffiti: "COVID-19 WAS HERE". 96

Figure 6.1: Becoming Disabled. 108

Figure 6.2: A Near-Death Experience. 109

Table 1.1: Indicators of cases and deaths from COVID-19 in the world. 9

Table 2.1: Participants. 27

Table 7.1: Guiding Principles, Lessons Learned, Challenges Faced. 130

INTRODUCTION

Remembrance and an Ethics of Care: Living After the Event of the Pandemic's Coming into Being

James Salvo

When there are those to mourn us, there's always sadness in our death. However, what can be unmournable in relation to us at the time of our death can have to do with the way we might have lived. For instance, if we lived a life wherein we experienced forced and senseless suffering, at the time of our death such aspects of our life are unmournable. Such forced and senseless suffering isn't something that others can move on from by way of mourning, for such experiences cannot be undone for the sufferer, and a lived experience of comfort isn't available to the dead. Those who mourn, mourn what's meaningful and transform their relation to this meaning. The relation transforms from a meaningful relation to what had been into a meaningful relation to what is no longer. Literally speaking, then, forced and senseless suffering is unmournable because the senseless itself is without meaning. Still, the deaths of those who've suffered without meaning can themselves bring meaning to those who survive. At the very least, such deaths should mean to the surviving that redoubled efforts must be made such that in the future, no one is made to live experiences of forced and senseless suffering. While this isn't to imply that those who lived experiences of forced and senseless suffering are a means to an end—that one lived to serve as a mere reminder when one dies—the meaning of a continued need for justice mustn't ever be forgotten by those who live.

Deadly pandemics necessarily have death as a fundamental quality. When written out explicitly in this way, this is quite plain. However, I feel as though this plainness is somehow forgotten when my newsfeed updates me with COVID-19 death tolls as a matter of quotidian fare, alongside things such as stock market updates and reviews of the latest Marvel film.

As I said, I maintain that when there are those to mourn us, deaths are always sad, whether these deaths be the result of a pandemic or otherwise. And while it's true that not all people who died as the result of the pandemic lived lives of forced and senseless suffering, it is true that the pandemic disproportionately affected whole populations who experience forced and senseless suffering, killing many within these populations, at times because adequate health care was unavailable and equity regarding vaccine distribution was completely absent. Again, people are never a mere means to an end—lives are never simply a reminder—but we mustn't forget that for many who are experiencing forced and senseless suffering in their lives already, the meaning of the concept of pandemic isn't simply a set of inconveniences, but death.

Still, death itself—any death—is made meaningful only in relation to life. Thus, to frame the pandemic solely in terms of death is incomplete. Though we're all mortal, we aren't simply beings for death, but beings who seek to live and flourish. And in this sense we should question what it means to live through the pandemic and to live after the event of the pandemic. At the time of this writing, the pandemic is ongoing; either it will end or it won't. In either case, the event of the pandemic coming into being has come to pass, and in this sense, life after this event is always already post-pandemic life. This doesn't necessarily imply that the pandemic is either over or ongoing, only that the pandemic was something that happened, something that's an event inasmuch as it puts subsequent living on a course that would've been otherwise had the pandemic never occurred. In this way, we won't ever *not* be post-pandemic—until, that is, the pandemic is forgotten. Should the pandemic ever be forgotten? I don't purport to know. However, I do believe that any lessons we've learned from the pandemic that continue to have importance shouldn't be forgotten, for we'll only have to learn them again.

One lesson that we've habitually relearned from the pandemic is that we as individuals can face struggles with regard to our own personal flourishing, but the magnitude of these struggles—no matter how great—mustn't let us forget that others, too, struggle, and this latter fact alone doesn't allow any one individual to rest once their own flourishing seems set. We may breathe a sigh of relief, but that's only to catch our breath so that we may help others find the means to flourish themselves. Sadly, we've learned such a lesson negatively, as many of us witnessed how certain individuals refused to mask or get vaccinated for no reason other than to express their own personal freedom, and this expression had absolutely no regard for the safety and well-being of others.

And if, in recent years, the dearly paid price of learning and relearning any lessons we have was all the sufferings and deaths—some unavoidable, others not—associated with the pandemic, we ought to make an effort not to simply *not* forget these lessons, but to remember with purpose. Not forgetting and remembering with purpose, of course, aren't necessarily the same thing. We purposively remember lessons through the practices of education, and it's in this spirit that the chapters in this volume sit at the intersection of the pandemic and the educational. The chapters contained herein seek to provide responses to the question not only of what it's meant to live through the pandemic, but what it will mean to live after the event of the pandemic, to live and flourish through an ethics of care by contextualizing and remembering the lessons we've learned.

Chapter Summaries

In Chapter 1, Edith J. Cisneros-Cohernour, Roger J. González-González, and Karla E. Atoche-Rodríguez discuss the teaching of qualitative research to students from different disciplinary backgrounds in Mexico, noting in particular how qualitative research emphasizes the importance of social context and understanding the communities in which one works and researches. They make note of how these contextual understandings are important for the future of qualitative researchers, especially when those contexts involve inequality made more acute since the pandemic.

Moving to the context of ethical concerns, in Chapter 2, Jill Channing and Georgina Wilson call attention to how individuals are shaped through relational learning and the importance of creating a climate of care based upon the principles of care ethics. They apply this idea to inquiring how educational leadership educators maintained a climate of caring during the pandemic in a classroom setting.

Continuing on the theme of care, in Chapter 3, Ciro De Vincenzo, Anita Franceschi, and Monica Massari examine a project that could be taken in the context of necessary self-care during the pandemic. They address a case study of the "Viral Epistolary" (VE) collective writing project. The aim of VE was the creation of an online space for sharing perspectives related to the experiences of domestic isolation, physical distancing, and quarantine during the pandemic. It used the "epistolary genre as a mediation, meaning-making, and auto-biographical tool."

Chapter 4 further explores a climate of caring and the online as an educational space. Ezequiel Korin writes about how to support students outside the physical classroom space. Examining Short Messaging Service (SMS) as a pedagogical tool, Korin notes that "Despite its many flaws and somewhat questionable flattening of the instructor–learner relationship, short text messages provide an effective route for students to feel seen, looked after, and to seek help whenever the more conventional mechanisms of institutional dialogue fall short."

Documents of personal experience of the pandemic are of great importance for preserving lessons learned during the pandemic. In Chapter 5, Aravindhan Natarajan gives us an exemplar of this through his arts-based personal narrative and sketchbook excerpts. In Chapter 6, Carol Rogers-Shaw shares with us "the double-sided nature of completing a dissertation during a pandemic," sharing both the immensity of the challenges and the joys of productive and meaningful work. In Chapter 7, Cathy Raymond shares reflections on her dissertation research, "a qualitative cross-cultural feminist research project conducted entirely online from February 2019 until February 2021 with Parvana, an Afghan woman who was living in Afghanistan until August 2021." Raymond further observes that "Despite the many challenges posed by the ongoing pandemic—challenges which continue to disrupt our everyday lives and professional undertakings—engaging in online cross-cultural research with an open mind, imagination, and care offers researchers opportunities for developing creative, collaborative, and flexible approaches to knowledge production which can not only circumvent challenges posed by a pandemic but also simultaneously result in more equitable and respectful research practices."

Chapter 8 concludes the present volume with the importance of remembrance not only as it pertains to education, but also to social justice inquiry in general, especially in the context of the pandemic. Emina Buzinkic endeavors to "move us towards the mobilization of the new ways of knowledge production that unsettle scarring working of racialized criminalization and cultural exclusions," discussing the labor of sharing life stories of refugee youth from South West Asia and North Africa through collective memory writing.

In the context of the living taking place after the pandemic's coming into being as an event, this volume humbly offers these writings as documents of remembrance of our historical present, with the hope that the historical may continue to move forward with an ethics of care ever in the foreground.

ONE

Teaching and Learning of Qualitative Research in Times of COVID-19 in Mexico

Edith J. Cisneros-Cohernour, Roger J. González-González, and Karla E. Atoche-Rodríguez

Introduction

IN DECEMBER 2019, CHINA REPORTED the first case of coronavirus (COVID-19), which later spread rapidly and resulted in an enormous number of deaths worldwide. As a result of the pandemic, changes were enacted, and new approaches were initiated around the globe related to health, economy, technologies, education, and so on. In the case of Mexico, government authorities mandated confinement and restricted jobs and services to prevent the spread of the virus (Escudero et al., 2020). The confinement also affected the educational system at all levels.

By March 2020, the Mexican Department of Education ordered the closure of all educational institutions in the country and established the program *Learn at Home* for teaching basic education (K–12), special education, and adult education students. Some schools also provided online education. According to the Inter-American Development Bank (IDB, 2020), Mexican teachers gained access to an extensive digital library that provided educational materials, workbooks, and even educational games for children. In addition, the Department of Education provided training for teachers and school administrators.

Mexican universities organized their own training programs for faculty and began to offer online education to their students. The change from face-to-face teaching to emergency remote instruction was difficult for faculty and students, particularly for those facing limited access to technology and experiencing problems with digital connectivity (Zapata-Garibay et al., 2021).

The university at which our study took place also faced limitations, particularly with students attending the campus located at the eastern end of the state, as well as students from low-income families on the campus at the state capital. The institution conducted surveys among faculty and students in order to help make decisions about how to provide better access to education to students who faced those conditions, as well as about returning to face-to-face instruction by the end of 2020.

Results of the survey indicated that most students opposed the return because they feared contagion, particularly those using public transportation to attend the university. Other students were concerned about infecting family members who were vulnerable because of their health status or did not want to attend face-to-face instruction until an effective treatment for COVID-19 became available. There were also some students who stated that online teaching was flawed, because they felt that this type of instruction did not allow them to assuage their doubts and understand the topics in great depth, but they agreed with online teaching because of safety concerns. For these reasons, the university continued with online instruction until the end of 2021.

In this chapter, we present our experience teaching a qualitative graduate course at a university in southern Mexico. The course began in January 2020, two months before the beginning of the confinement in Mexico and lasted until June of that year. During that semester, six students registered for our course, all of whom were in their second year of their doctoral program and came from different disciplinary backgrounds in the social sciences. The nine students were comprised of five women and four men.

Literature Review

The COVID-19 pandemic has had a significant impact on the multiple sectors that constitute our societies and has generated uncertainty, fear, and anguish among people (Johnson et al., 2020). Humanity has faced a series of challenges in matters of health, economy, social development, and education that has resulted in the looting and marginalization of the working class (Minoldo & Dvoskin, 2021). The pandemic has caused a serious economic recession worldwide (Zúñiga et al., 2020), one that has revealed the brutal structural gaps in the economic and social sectors (Bárcena, 2020). In a capitalist and globalized economy, the confinement has made evident these consequences of an economic race aimed at both accumulation of wealth and economic development (Sen, 1999). The focus has been on increasing wealth, which has generated a growing inequality among different countries (World Bank, 2020).

Based on the indicators of the World Health Organization (WHO, 2022), there have been a total of 503,131,834 cases of COVID-19 across the world. Table 1.1 shows that the regions most affected by the pandemic have been Europe and the Americas, with the latter having experienced the greater impact. In terms of total deaths, the World Health Organization reports a combined total of more than two million deaths on the two American continents, a figure much higher than that of other regions, including Europe.

Table 1.1. Indicators of cases and deaths from COVID-19 in the world

World Health Organization Region	Accumulated Cases	Total Accumulated Deaths
Europe	210,770,575	1,968,472
Americas	152,012,590	2,715,048
South-East Asia	57,613,528	782,492
Western Pacific	52,375,616	212,224
Eastern Mediterranean	21,673,983	341,902
Africa	8,684,778	171,420

Source: Adapted from the World Health Organization (2022).

As Table 1 shows, even though more cases of COVID-19 have been registered in other regions of the world, there are different contextual variables in the Americas that drive the higher number of deaths. In this sense the health emergency has been synonymous with the economic and social emergency (Martínez Franzoni & Sánchez Ancochea, 2022), generating a setback of at least a decade in the region (Economic Commission for Latin America and the Caribbean [ECLAC], 2021) and exacerbating the influence of the pandemic, especially in areas such as education and scientific research (World Bank, 2020).

Education, Research, and COVID-19

The disruption of face-to-face education due to the pandemic has impacted 1.6 billion students in 190 countries, or 94% of students in the world. That figure rises to 99% in countries that lag economically, resulting in the greatest crisis in the history of educational systems across the world (United Nations,

2020). Given this scenario, the pandemic has posed formidable challenges to governments, their policies, and educational systems in general. These can be summarized as follows:

1. At the beginning of the pandemic in March 2020, the main challenge was to continue with distance learning processes, considering the closure of classrooms and the change from face-to-face educational systems to non-face-to-face modalities. This was to be achieved mainly through digital resources, technological platforms, and autonomous learning in response to the demands of social distancing, but which also highlighted the social, economic, and access-to-knowledge asymmetries between those who do and those who do not have access to these emerging modalities.
2. The end of 2021 witnessed the beginning of the return to classrooms and the design of training strategies based on hybrid models, as well as the alternation between face-to-face and virtual strategies, which has represented a second great challenge for educational systems.
3. In addition, given the current scenario and the two years' worth of social distancing in schools, we note a third challenge that educational systems currently face or are about to face. This challenge is represented by socio-affective problems and emotional development that the children and young people of the world face today because of two years of confinement during the pandemic.
4. Finally, there is the challenge facing the teaching processes and learning methodologies to produce scientific knowledge exploring multiple realities and phenomena that were confronted in social and educational contexts, and that have traditionally been studied through qualitative research. We offer this last challenge as a trigger for the study of the relationship between teaching-learning processes, qualitative research, and COVID-19 that we address in this chapter.

As is traditional in the academic field, scientific, social, and educational research processes represent one of the fundamental bases for development and contribute to overcoming the problems faced by humanity (Gonzalo-Eslava, 2018). Thus, in the face of the pandemic, the development of research, particularly socio-educational research, has faced a variety of challenges that

Colás-Bravo (2021) summarizes as: (a) the relationship between information and communication technologies (ICTs) and education; (b) education for a sustainable world; and (c) research training.

The pandemic strengthened the relationship between ICTs and education to the point of turning technology into a channel through which training processes can be accessed from home, becoming a support for teaching and learning processes in these times.

Over the years, a high-demand field for educational and social research has focused on this relationship (ICTs–educational processes). However, the emerging scenarios from the pandemic have called for new ways and strategies for doing research that not only focus on analyzing the relationship with technology, but also allow the use of these tools for the development of research in the educational field—thus becoming one more tool to which the researcher resorts, at the educational level of field diaries, questionnaires, and informed consents, to name a few.

The second challenge for research that Colás-Bravo poses is education for a sustainable world, an approach that coincides with the United Nations' 2030 Agenda and that seeks to "transform the dominant development paradigm into one that takes us along the path of sustainable, inclusive development with a long-term vision" (United Nations, 2018, p. 7). Thus, the social and educational research that is generated in the wake of the pandemic must produce knowledge that guarantees social well-being, inclusion, equity, and basic norms for sustainable development.

The last challenge to research has to do with the training of researchers. Given the profound problems that are currently experienced and the multiple social and educational needs, we believe we should move to qualitative perspectives that contemplate the sensitivity of the researcher, the holistic, comprehensive construction of knowledge perspectives all that is consistent with emerging realities.

This makes it necessary to approach the teaching-learning processes of qualitative research—which can be taught, internalized by students, and often understood, but which only materialize and make sense in the field, in the context and in the intersection of perceptions that allow real constructs to emerge. That is why the teaching and learning processes of qualitative research constitute a little-explored field, one that needs to be analyzed especially in these post-pandemic times, and one in which education and social development have already been transformed from the outset.

Teaching and Learning Qualitative Research in Times of COVID-19

Teaching and research in the academic field are two closely interrelated constructs that feed each other while generating knowledge. This relationship has historically been framed in a positivist, quantitative, and behavioral paradigm in terms of teaching, mainly because science, since its inception, has been based on an empirical-analytical perspective with a positivist approach to reality and causal explanations. However, the repercussions of the COVID-19 pandemic have not only had an impact on health and economic development issues, but have also caused endless social, educational, and emotional consequences that, as we have mentioned, need to be studied through qualitative methodologies.

It is in this context that it becomes relevant to talk about the teaching and learning process of qualitative research in times of pandemic, because through the analysis of the specialized literature, it has been found that the study of the teaching-learning relationship and qualitative research has been limited to the approach of educational methodologies such as project-oriented learning or problem-based learning, active and motivating methodologies that involve the student in learning knowledge and skills through an extended process of inquiry (UNICEF, 2020). This is particularly the case in basic education, without considering approaches such as that of Bourdieu and fellow researchers, who affirm that one learns to do research only by researching, and that qualitative research is an interpretive process that examines human and social problems (Creswell, 1998), which makes it necessary to be taught through real scenarios and tools.

A Qualitative Course in Times of COVID-19

From January to the first days of March 2020, the class met once a week in a classroom located in the heart of the socioeconomic-administrative and humanities campus situated in the eastern part of the city. Beginning on March 15, the course continued online until the end of June of that year. The classroom had two large windows and good lighting. There was a blackboard in front of the room and tables and chairs for twenty students in the rectangular-shaped classroom. Students were usually on time when the classes were face-to-face, but they often arrived 10 or 15 minutes late when the classes moved online.

As part of the course, they were required to develop a research project using a qualitative design. They engaged in different activities related to the project, such as conducting interviews, on-site observations, focus groups, document analysis, as well as the scrutiny of different qualitative study reports.

All students were asked to comply with the university policy established during the time of the confinement that limited field research and requested them to sign a letter consenting to voluntarily participation in field practices during the contingency and releasing the university from facts or circumstances raised during fieldwork that might compromise their physical and/or patrimonial integrity, as well as that of third parties, as a consequence of failure to comply with health and other applicable regulations.

Challenges

During the semester in question, students faced different challenges, some of them related to preconceptions about the course, the difficulty of shifting to a different frame of mind, and understanding the complexities of qualitative research and the difficulties of obtaining information from the participants of the study, due in part to the conditions of the confinement.

Difficulty Moving to a Different Perspective and Understanding Qualitative Research

Some students had no prior preparation in qualitative research. Their idea of a qualitative study was conducting interviews or focus groups, and they struggled to understand how to identify the issues in a qualitative project. As one student stated:

> The main challenge that I faced was opening my mind to new ways of working and implementing research methodologies. Personally, it has caused me a lot of work to write critical issues. I consider that I still have not achieved this as I want, but I am more aware of my limitations.

Another student added:

> It was complicated for me to pass from a quantitative to a qualitative perspective. I had taken courses on data analysis, but never had prior experience on how to conduct a qualitative study or how to design a qualitative proposal.

Other students expressed that a qualitative study was complex and required more from them than what they had expected:

> It is a new kind of research for me, it demanded a lot of time and detail. At the beginning I thought qualitative research was about using interviews, but later I learned that it was more complex. It was also hard for me to illustrate my learning with my project.

Difficulties in Obtaining Information from the Participants of the Study

Some students experienced problems because of the conditions for conducting the study during the confinement and the problems related to work and study from home. As one student stated:

> One of the main challenges for me was the pandemic, it was difficult to work at home when all the members (of the family) were there at the same time, there was only one computer, and we all needed to use it.

Another student added:

> At the beginning I was able to visit the organization that I was studying; then the confinement started. I had to work and study from home. There were connectivity problems. At the end, I became physically and mentally exhausted.

Other students referred to the lack of access to the places where they were conducting their project, difficulty accessing the participants of the study, and using some techniques, such as observation, during the pandemic. As one student commented:

> One problem that I faced was the complexity of obtaining information (data) and contacting participants for interviews and observations due to the current pandemic contingency.

Another student, who designed her study in a rural community in the state, added:

> I lacked time to do interviews due to the schedules of the subjects that I was going to interview and the distance from where they were. Not all of them had a cell phone.

As instructors, we also recognized that students had problems adapting from face-to-face to online teaching at the beginning of the course. Some of them joined their peers from a more advanced class in requesting that their tuition be waived because "online teaching was not real teaching." Although the university had provided online training to the faculty, and all students were recipients of a fellowship from the Mexican Council for Science and Technology, they were not content with using those resources to pay for internet services and missed social interaction.

Projects

Despite these circumstances and challenges, students were able to complete their projects and learn about qualitative research. As part of the course, they developed the following projects:

1. Case study of a student facing family violence during the contingency due to COVID-19. This study was conducted by Casanova (2021), a teacher who began to teach online classes because of the pandemic. She noticed that some of her students reduced their participation in class, particularly a young teenager named Carmen. After obtaining permission from the student and her family, she began to conduct a case study about how Carmen and her family had dealt with the changes in daily life since the beginning of their confinement. Casanova conducted in-depth interviews with Carmen, her mother, her brothers, and her father. She also interviewed some of her instructors. Through her study, she learned that because of the confinement, one of Carmen's brothers had lost his job and moved back into the family house. This situation became very stressful because of his consumption of marijuana and his confrontations with his father, who was an alcoholic. Carmen found herself affected by the stress, her loss of autonomy, and her mother, who was exhausted from trying to juggle her work, home activities, and the children. The case study allowed Casanova to learn how the pandemic had created situations that increased family problems related to mental and physical health, economics, and violence.
2. Life histories of drivers working for Uber during the contingency. Ramírez (2021) conducted a study about the experiences of Uber drivers during the pandemic. He was a former employee of that company

and was interested in how changes in the context affected the work of the drivers, given new government policies imposing taxes on Uber and similar companies providing transportation options in the city. Through document analysis, interviews with drivers and clients, as well as participating in a WhatsApp group, he learned the problems experienced by the drivers, as their income was reduced because of the company's new policies and the mandated confinement in the city.

3. Sustainability and Beekeeping: Management challenges in the honey industry in southern Mexico. Gamiño (2021) examined the challenges faced by the management of a honey-producing company due to external issues that threatened the survival of the business. Data collection involved on-site observations, interviews, document analysis, and focus group interviews with different actors. According to the findings, there were issues related to auditing, logistics, and administrative problems because of new government policies that the Department of Agriculture and Rural Development have imposed. In addition, the author identified other challenges faced by family business managers with no management background, the effects of climate change on beekeeping, and the great damage that is causing the indiscriminate use of agrochemicals in the production and quality of honey.
4. Leadership challenges faced in providing education in a rural, marginalized community: the case study of a private university in southern Mexico. In this project, Ortíz (2021) conducted a study on a private institution that opened a new center for higher education in a rural town in southern Mexico. He focused on the following question: To what extent are the management and leadership strategies contributing to (a) the educational inclusion of young people living in poverty; (b) economic improvement and social development in the town; and (c) the promotion of leadership aptitude among their students? He collected data through interviews, observations, and documentary analysis. Most of the data collection took place face-to-face, but in the end, he included online interviews and focus groups.
5. A project on the resilience of musicians in training. In this project, Contreras (2021) focused on examining the challenges faced by students from a musical center in southeastern Mexico, both in their training and on a personal level. In the course of the study, he learned that students

developed resilience in the face of adversity, stress management, unforeseen situations, and personal, work, and emotional situations that affected their studies and personal lives. Data collection involved interviews, documentary analysis, and observations. He contrasted the findings of his project with other studies related to musical training in Mexico and other countries.

6. The last project focused on the effects of work on women in a rural community due to the establishment of a new water treatment plant in the community. In this project, Palma (2021) wanted to examine the changes that occurred in the community because of the new water treatment plant, and how the urbanization of the town affected rural families, particularly women and their work. At the beginning of the course, Palma was able to conduct some interviews with the families, but she had problems collecting data, since the town limited access to visitors during the pandemic.

During the course, we used plenary sessions as opportunities for students to reflect on their role as researchers, their ethical performance accessing the site and the participants, and their conducting of their study. We also emphasized the importance of interpretive validity in the development of their work. After the course was completed, they shared with us some of what they learned, but stated that they would have preferred that the conditions had allowed for more time in the field. As one student stated:

> I think the course has been very helpful; it has given me a new look at qualitative research. However, I wish I had more time for conducting observations. I think it would have helped me formulate the critical questions better. I know how to do it now, if I only had more time observing the families. . . .

Conclusions

In particular, the pandemic caused by SARS-CoV2 (COVID-19) has generated a series of changes in the educational field, giving rise to the experience of an emerging remote education (ERE) defined by Hodges et al. (2020)—in particular, the instruction that is given during an emergency or crisis, in which alternative methods and means are used to temporarily remedy the lack of face-to-face teaching with the available resources. ERE is a first indicator of the type of education that will finally be promoted in the face of the emergency, which is commonly oriented toward distance education, online classes, and virtual classes. For their part, Vera Caicedo and Loaiza Zuluaga (2015) define an emerging education as that educational process that takes place even in situations of risk (war, health conditions, or natural disasters) that cause suspension of work in schools and significant changes in the educational system, both of which interfere in the pedagogical process.

In the case of teaching qualitative research, the pandemic affected both the way we were able to teach and the work of students during their preparation. This chapter has described our finding that our students were able to work on their projects partly because most of them began those projects two months before the confinement. Some of them relied more on the use of information and communication technologies for collecting their data, such as those recommended by proponents of designs such as Digital Ethnography (Pink et al., 2016), Virtual Ethnography (Hine, 2015), or Netnography (Kozinets, 2015), to mention a few, as well as scenarios in which the phenomenon is built through virtual interactions such as social networks, platforms, blogs, and others. Some used virtual interviews, as recommended by Salmons (2012), and online focus groups (Lathen & Laestadius, 2021), among other tools for collecting information during the confinement.

We agree with Thakur et al. (2020), United Nations (2020), and Amadasun (2021), that the use of information and communication technologies, techniques, and methods has allowed for the collection of valuable information during the pandemic. However, that approach has also brought new, critical issues for qualitative research, such as the reluctance of some research participants to engage in interviews and focus groups, and the very limited access to technology by the poor and indigenous population of the country. As the National Institute of Statistics and Geography (INEG, 2018) has shown, in Mexico only 44.3% of the households have computers in their homes, while most homes located in rural communities with a high percentage of indigenous population are in poverty and lack this access.

In addition, it is essential to remember that qualitative research is nourished by the approach of the researcher to the social context. Said approach feeds on voices, interactions, impressions, feelings, and a close relationship with field work and observation. Thus, for its teaching, we require the process that utilizes real research scenarios, which allows for the appropriation of concepts and contents from the field, considering that qualitative research is by itself interpretive and is guided by a set of experiences, beliefs, and feelings about the context and how it must be understood, studied, and taught (Guba, 1990; Denzin & Lincoln, 2018).

Finally, we believe that despite the pandemic, students were able to live the experience and learn about qualitative research. Having started their projects before the confinement gave them opportunities: first, to become immersed in their study and to obtain a better understanding of the communities in which they worked, and second, to reflect on the impact of the context once they lost access to the sites and had to redesign their work to complete their studies. A deep understanding of the context is essential for future qualitative researchers, especially in Mexico, a country marked by socio-cultural and equality challenges that have become more acute since the onset of the pandemic. In our course, students conducted studies in the southeast of Mexico, where the indigenous population faces multiple social, economic, and cultural problems, including marginalization and educational backwardness (Mijangos et al., 2009).

References

Amadasun, S. (2021). COVID-19 pandemic in Africa: What lessons for social work education and practice? *International Social Work, 64*(2), 246–250. https://doi.org/10.1177/0020872820949620

Bárcena, A. (2020). *Los efectos económicos y sociales del COVID-19 en América Latina y el Caribe.* Naciones Unidas. https://www.cepal.org/sites/default/files/presentation/files/200605_final_presentacion_parlamericasv_alicia_barcena.pdf

Bourdieu, P., Chamboredon, J. C., & Passeron, J. C. (2002). *El oficio del sociólogo, presupuestos epistemológicos.* Siglo XXI editores.

Casanova, J. A. (2021). *Cambios en la cotidianidad de las familias por la contingencia del COVID-19. El caso de Alicia.* Unpublished project report. Universidad Autónoma de Yucatán.

Colás-Bravo, P. (2021). Retos de la investigación educativa tras la pandemia COVID-19. *Revista de Investigación Educativa, 39*(2), 319–333. http://dx.doi.org/10.6018/rie.469871

Contreras, G. (2021). *Resiliencia de músicos en formación: Un estudio de caso.* Unpublished project report. Universidad Autónoma de Yucatán.

Creswell, J. W. (1998). *Qualitative inquiry and research design: Choosing among five traditions.* Sage.

Denzin, N. K., & Lincoln, Y. S. (2018). Introduction: The discipline and practice of qualitative research. In N. K. Denzin & Y. S. Lincoln (Eds.), *The SAGE handbook of qualitative research* (pp. 29–71). Sage.

Economic Commission for Latin America and the Caribbean. (2021). *Panorama social de América Latina*. Naciones Unidas. https://repositorio.cepal.org/bitstream/handle/11362/47718/1/S2100655_es.pdf

Escudero, X., Guarner, J., Galindo, A., Escudero-Salamanca, M., Alcocer, M., & Del Rio, C. (2020). La pandemia de coronavirus SARS-CoV-2 (COVID-19): Situación actuales implicaciones para México. *Cardiovascular and Metabolic Science, 31*(3), 170–177. https://dx.doi.org/10.35366/93943

Gamiño, M. (2021). *Cambio climático, Cuarta transformación sustentabilidad y apicultura: Retos de una gestión en la industria de la miel*. Unpublished project report. Universidad Autónoma de Yucatán.

Gonzalo-Eslava, D. (2018). La función social de la investigación. *Investigaciones Andina, 20*(36), 5–8. https://www.redalyc.org/articulo.oa?id=239059788001

Guba, E. G. (1990). The alternative paradigm dialog. In E. G. Guba (Ed.), *The paradigm dialog* (pp. 17–30). Sage.

Hine, C. (2015). *Ethnography for the Internet: Embedded, embodied and everyday*. Routledge.

Hodges, C., Moore, S., Lockee, B., Trust, T., & Bond, A. (2020). The difference between emergency remote teaching and online learning. *EDUCAUSE Review*. https://er.educause.edu/articles/2020/3/the-difference-between-emergency-remote-teaching-and-online-learning

Instituto Nacional de Estadística y Geografía. (2018). *Encuesta nacional sobre disponibilidad y uso de tecnologías de la información en los hogares 2018*. México.

Inter-American Bank of Development. (2020). *La educación en tiempos del coronavirus: Los sistemas educativos de América Latina y el Caribe ante COVID-19*. https://publications.iadb.org/es/la-educacion-en-tiempos-del-coronavirus-los-sistemas-educativos-de-america-latina-y-el-caribe-ante-covid-19

Johnson, M. C., Saletti-Cuesta, L., & Tumas, N. (2020). Emociones, preocupaciones y reflexiones frente a la pandemia del COVID-19 en Argentina. *Ciência & Saúde Coletiva, 25*, 2447–2456. 10.1590/1413-81232020256.1.10472020.

Kozinets, R. (2015). *Netnography: Redefined*. Sage.

Lathen, L., & Laestadius, L. (2021). Reflections on online focus group research with low socioeconomic status African American adults during COVID-19. *International Journal of Qualitative Methods, 20*, 1–10. https://doi.org/10.1177/16094069211021713

Martínez Franzoni, J., & Sánchez Ancochea, D. (2022). *¿Puede la COVID-19 avanzar la política social inclusiva? Las transferencias monetarias de emergencia en Centroamérica*. Fundación Carolina–UNESCO. https://www.fundacioncarolina.es/wp-content/uploads/2022/01/DT_FC_60.pdf

Mijangos, J. C., Canto, P. J., & Cisneros, E. J. (2009). Introducción. In Mijangos, J.C. (Ed.), *La lucha contra el rezago educativo: El caso de los mayas en Yucatán* (pp. 9–44). Unas Letras Industria Editorial.

Minoldo, S., & Dvoskin, N. (2021). *El desafío social en tiempos de pandemia. ¿Cambios estructurales en los regímenes de bienestar?* Fundación Friedrich Ebert. https://www.clacso.org/wp-content/uploads/2021/07/El-desafio-social-en-tiempos-de-pandemia.pdf

Ortíz, J. C. (2021). *El ejercicio del liderazgo en una universidad al sur del Estado de Yucatán.* Unpublished project report. Universidad Autónoma de Yucatán.

Palma, Y. (2021). *El trabajo de las mujeres rurales de la comisaría de San Ignacio Tesip, Mérida, Yucatán, México.* Unpublished project report. Universidad Autónoma de Yucatán.

Pink, S., Horst, H., Postill, J., Hjorth, L., Lewis, T., & Tacchi, J. (2016). *Digital ethnography: Principles and practice.* Sage.

Ramírez, N. (2021). *Comprendiendo el fenómeno uber y el costo de su flexibilidad laboral.* Unpublished project report. Universidad Autónoma de Yucatán.

Salmons, J. (2012). *Cases in online interview research.* Sage.

Sen, A. (1999). *Development as freedom.* Anchor Books.

Thakur, K., Kumar, N., & Sharma, N. (2020). Effect of the pandemic and lockdown on mental health of children. *Indian Journal of Pediatrics, 87*(7), 552. https://doi.org/10.1007/s12098-020-03308-w

UNICEF. (2020). *El aprendizaje basado en proyectos en PLANEA.* Naciones Unidas. https://www.unicef.org/argentina/media/7771/file

United Nations. (2018). *La Agenda 2030 y los Objetivos de Desarrollo Sostenible: Una oportunidad para América Latina y el Caribe.* https://repositorio.cepal.org/bitstream/handle/11362/40155/24/S1801141_es.pdf

United Nations. (2020). *Informe de políticas: La COVID-19 y la necesidad de actuar en relación con la salud mental.* https://www.un.org/sites/un2.un.org/files/policy_brief_-_covid_and_mental_health_spanish.pdf

Vera Caicedo, K., & Loaiza Zuluaga, Y. E. (2015). Educación en emergencias o emergencias en educación. *Plumilla Educativa, 16*(2), 324–341. https://doi.org/10.30554/plumillaedu.16.1614.2015

World Bank. (2020). *COVID-19: Impacto en la educación y respuestas de política pública.* Grupo Banco Mundial, educación. https://thedocs.worldbank.org/en/doc/143771590756983343-0090022020/original/Covid19EducationSummaryesp.pdf

World Health Organization. (2022). *Coronavirus (COVID-19) dashboard: Situation by region, country, territory & area.* WHO. https://covid19.who.int/table

Zapata-Garibay, R., González-Fogoaga, J. E., Meza-Rodríguez, E., Salazar-Ramírez, E., Plascencia-López, I., & González-Fogoaga, C. J. (2021). Mexico's higher education students' experience during the lockdown due to the COVID-19 pandemic. *Frontiers Education, 6*, 1–13. https://doi.org/10.3389/feduc.2021.683222

Zúñiga, L. M., Restrepo, L. C., Osorio, R. C., Buendía, J. C., & Muñoz, H. (2020). La economía global en tiempo de crisis del COVID-19. *Revista Espacios, 41*(42), 381–387. 10.48082/espacios-a20v41n42p33.

TWO

"They Could Count on Me": Educational Leadership Educators' Development of a Culture of Caring During the COVID-19 Pandemic

Jill Channing and Georgina E. Wilson

THE 2020 GLOBAL COVID-19 PANDEMIC caused a change in the basic assumptions about the ways educators interact with their students at every educational level from early childhood to graduate school. As a result, both educators and students alike are experiencing heightened levels of anxiety and stress surrounding distance learning in the wake of the pandemic, leading to increased workloads, student disengagement, and educator burnout (Eadie et al., 2021; Hoyt et al., 2021; Liu et al., 2021; Madrigal & Blevins, 2021). Additionally, this shift from past interaction practices creates significant barriers for educators working with marginalized populations, including refugees (Häggström et al., 2020; Primdahl et al., 2020), and students with disabilities (Valicenti-McDermott et al., 2022).

Previous research has shown that educators who model behaviors that create a climate of caring and self-belonging in the classroom tend to have a higher rate of student engagement and report increased professional quality of life and well-being (Anderson et al., 2021; DeMartino, 2021). The creation of a climate of care is based on care ethics, which holds that individuals are shaped through relational learning (Held, 2006). Within the context of education, the educator takes on the role of caretaker, and the student takes on the role of the cared-for. This dialogic process allows the student to learn what it means to be cared for and can later model the caring role (Noddings, 2012; Page, 2018). Similarly, Goldstein (1998) clarified that implementing care strategies in the classroom extends beyond empathy, and instead consists of reciprocal relationships involving motivational displacement and engrossment. Likewise, research suggests that employing care-based classroom management systems over traditional punishment-and-reward classroom management systems modeled relational empathy and camaraderie among students (Rabin, 2016). Research has shown that educators who facilitate a climate of caring by placing expectations on students and showing a genuine interest in their achievement and learning leads to higher student achievement, high affective feelings of success, and positive regard for teachers (Hawk, 2017; Johnston et al., 2022). As a result, current evidence suggests that fostering a climate of caring is essential to the moral development and academic success of students.

Overall, the current research surrounding creating a climate of caring during the COVID-19 pandemic is still limited (Berry, 2020; Eveleigh et al., 2022; Sorrells & Madrid Akpovo, 2022), and the research related to practicing the ethics of caring in educational leadership classrooms is sparse (Berkovich & Eyal, 2020; Gerstl-Pepin et al., 2006). However, researchers agree that the COVID-19 pandemic creates an opportunity to foster a culture of care and refocus on what is most important, and in doing so make academic practice more respectful and relationship-focused (Corbera et al., 2020). Educators have implemented social and emotional learning (SEL) strategies in the classroom, which align with fostering a climate of caring. Likewise, evidence suggests that the implementation of social and emotional learning skills during the pandemic increased measures of social and emotional well-being, including mental health and academic performance (Zieher et al., 2021). Social and emotional learning emphasizes the importance of learning skills such as collaboration, conflict resolution, and perspective-taking in long-term health promotion and educational attainment (Elias & Weissberg, 2000). A meta-analysis consisting of 213 studies revealed that social and emotional learning programs yielded increased pro-social behaviors, improved academic achievement, and reduced behavioral conduct issues and levels of internalizing symptoms (Durlak et al., 2011). Evidence suggests that educators who have higher levels of self-efficacy report lower levels of exhaustion, even during distance learning education (Soncini et al., 2021). Research has found that educators with higher levels of competency in social and emotional learning report higher levels of educator self-efficacy and less compassion fatigue (Yang, 2021). The purpose of the qualitative study's phenomenological inquiry was to understand the ways in which educational leadership teachers navigated the complex challenges of meeting their students' needs during the pandemic and the ways in which they cultivated and maintained a climate of caring in their often-virtual classrooms.

Literature Review

The use of ethical (Berkovich & Eyal, 2020; Gerstl-Pepin et al., 2006), philosophical (Brown, 2004; Cambron-McCabe & McCarthy, 2005; Capper et al., 2006; McClellan & Dominguez, 2006), and values education in educational leadership preparation programs (Berkovich, 2017; Furman, 2012; McKenzie et al., 2008) has long been studied. Berkovich and Eyal (2020) studied an educational leadership program in Israel for six years, during which time they developed pre- and post-test instruments to measure ethical development. They found that ethics education has limited effects, as determined by their instruments. However, when the student participants were grouped by those who did change their ethical views and those who did not, significant differences in ethical viewpoints emerged, suggesting that educational leadership instruction on ethics and identity formation can lead to varying outcomes, depending on the students' openness to values-based education. Gerstl-Pepin and fellow researchers (2006) studied an educational leadership preparation program with ethics education embedded throughout its curriculum and values, ethics, and social justice education as part of its mission and vision statements. In cohorts, students developed commitments to an ethics of caring as part of their student-created group expectations. However, the instructors in this program became concerned that the ethics commitments were grounded in a sense of color-blindness, reflecting a lack of recognition, on the students' part, of systemic racism and oppression embedded in all U.S. social institutions. Through intentional social justice and ethical education, researchers learned that faculty members were effective in their teaching of diversity and equity issues, but survey responses revealed that social justice, multiculturalism, and diversity were not embedded in the curriculum but were instead taught distinctly. Therefore, these ethical concerns were marginalized within the curriculum, which is a finding echoed by Sleeter (1996). The researchers related this to the "whiteness" of their faculty, university, region, and state (Gerstl-Pepin et al., 2006). Gerstl-Pepin and colleagues (2006) recommended that "educational leadership programs must assess the racial norms that shape their curriculum, classroom practice, and interactions with students" and engage in faculty discussions to encourage further integration into the curricula (p. 262). Our study addresses the gaps in the literature on educational leadership professionals' perspectives on caring in the educational leadership classroom, caring strategies and purposes in the educational leadership classroom during the COVID-19 pandemic, and graduate–faculty-developed ethics of care frameworks.

Theoretical Framework

Nel Noddings (2012) and others have described care ethics in education as a moral philosophy that encourages relationship-development to further students' moral development and academic learning (Gilligan, 1982; Noddings, 1984). Educational ethics of care is described as contextual and relational perspectives on ethics (Bergmark, 2020; Noddings, 1984, 2012, 2013). Noddings (2012) emphasized that the carer is an attentive listener: "We must listen, not just 'tell,' assuming that we know what the other needs" (p. 773). Noddings (1984, 1992, 2012) argued that students must feel cared-for if they are to learn to care for others. She posited (2013) that reflection and communication are the prime methods for understanding others' perspectives and developing caring and trusting relationships. As our participants suggest throughout their narratives, they showed care for their students, helping them meet rigorous expectations and course objectives, as well as helping them develop caring attitudes and behaviors for others in their current and future leadership roles through reflection, discussion, and experiential learning activities.

Methodology

Using the phenomenological tradition, we aimed to develop inquiry methods that would assist us in identifying the essence of the lived experiences of educational leadership teachers during the COVID-19 pandemic (Creswell & Creswell, 2018; Riemen, 1986). In our results and findings, we constructed rich descriptions of the central phenomenon, exploring the research question: What are educational leadership professors' perceptions of work and life experiences during the COVID-19 pandemic? As Moustakas (1994) suggests, we asked about participants' experiences related to the central phenomenon and the contexts and situations in which they had these experiences.

We interviewed nine educational leadership instructors about their work and life experiences during the COVID-19 pandemic. In our construct of the pandemic period, we include current times (2022) as the pandemic period. We recruited participants by using public directory information, professional networks, and snowball sampling. The interviews were semi-structured to allow participants to share their experiences freely and to speak at length about the ways they navigated their work and lives during the pandemic. After completing interviews, we transcribed them, checking for accuracy. Then we began line-by-line coding, using first-order coding whereby we identified a variety of codes. After this step, we engaged in second-order coding, reducing the number of codes. We analyzed these second-order codes further and identified several emergent themes. We utilized ATLAS.ti to code and analyze data, utilizing a similar method as Varga and Paulus (2014) described:

> We used the qualitative data analysis software ATLAS.ti™ to systematize the analysis process, using the memo, comment, and coding features. After several cycles of analysis, we formed tentative interpretations of what the various discursive features were doing, moving back to the data to ground our claims. Finally, we selected representative excerpts from the data to demonstrate our findings through reworking of the analysis. (p. 445)

We wrote analytical and reflexive memos to ensure trustworthiness through our audit trailing detailing reactions, reflections, and analyses of these, and we shared our results with our participants so that they could provide feedback on our report. We also engaged in peer de-briefing as we identified emergent themes, including the following: the creation of caring spaces, the development of trusting student-teacher relationships, the effective facilitation of learning in the face of challenges, and mental health and wellness.

Participants

We interviewed nine educational leadership teachers from across the United States. Seven were women, and two were men. Four were people of color, two were Hispanic, and five were White.

Table 2.1. Participants

Gender (self-identified)	Race/ethnicity (self-identified)
7 Women	1 Person of Color, Hispanic
	2 Black, Non-Hispanic
	4 White, Non-Hispanic

Gender (self-identified)	Race/ethnicity (self-identified)
2 Men	1 White, Hispanic
	1 Black, Non-Hispanic

Reflexive Statements

Jill's Reflexive Statement and Role as Researcher

I am an educational leadership instructor and could relate to the participants whom Gina and I interviewed. I identify as non-binary Genderqueer with a Queer sexual orientation. I come from a working-class background, and I am a first-generation college student. My ethnicities are multiple. I engaged in analytical and reflective memoing to analyze and reflect upon my biases and preconceived notions about leadership learning and teaching during the pandemic. I appreciated that we had diverse participants from a variety of backgrounds, ethnicities, and regions throughout the United States. I saw my role as researcher to learn more about these educators' work and life experiences during the pandemic, recognizing that at the time of this research and this chapter writing (2022) the pandemic is still happening and affecting many aspects of faculty members' and students' lives. Likewise, I recognized the effects of the pandemic on my life, career, and teaching. Without focusing primarily on my own experiences for inspiration, I aimed to represent accurately the phenomenon of being an educational leadership instructor during the pandemic and to contribute uniquely to the field through this work, as no studies have been published addressing these educators' perceptions of teaching and students' leadership learning during the pandemic.

Gina's Reflexive Statement and Role as Researcher

I teach educational leadership and relate deeply to the participants we interviewed. I identify as a cis-gendered woman with a heterosexual orientation. I am the daughter of Mexican immigrants who broke the generational poverty cycle. I am a first-generation college student and a former PK–12 public school educator. I engaged in analytical and reflective memoing to consider, analyze, and reconcile any bias and preconceived notions that I had regarding teaching and learning in an educational leadership classroom, virtual teaching and learning, and teaching during the pandemic. I saw my role as a researcher as creating an opportunity for myself and the participants to learn more about their experiences during the COVID-19 pandemic as it related to their work as educators and to their lives. It was important for me to acknowledge that the pandemic is not over and that while we conducted interviews and are writing a chapter, many are still adversely affected by the pandemic. Although my own experiences of teaching during the pandemic created the initial wondering about how my colleagues were managing, the focus of the study is to give voice to the educational leadership instructors who served their students and to reflect and learn from what they put into praxis during that critical moment.

Findings

Creation of Caring Spaces

Participants explicitly narrated stories about caring classroom spaces during the pandemic. They described the communication and these spaces as "therapy sessions," "confessionals," and "therapy." Because the educator preparation professors who participated in the study were not clinically trained to provide therapy, these sessions may have felt therapeutic to students, but they cannot be considered therapy. Within these caring spaces, participants reported using the context of the pandemic as a teaching opportunity. "I didn't cut it short. I let them go, and we listened, and we talked about it. . . . I just tried to be more cognizant of letting them be who they are authentically." Students were allowed to vent and discuss being overwhelmed. Then they "decompressed and deconstructed that and really . . . tried to work through it." Another participant described this caring space as one "where we can be open, transparent, honest, and vulnerable." Noddings (2010, 2012) described a caring climate as one where educators develop caring relations, work to meet individual needs, provide supportive instruction, and encourage moral development, where the carer puts aside their own projects and priorities to *help*. All our participants were moral educators who spent class time talking about ethical problems and how to address these.

Participants described communication, often through Zoom or other video conferencing software, that enabled them to build class communities in which they would extend class time to have conversations "after class."

> I created extra space every time we were in community together to just share where they were and relate that to leadership however we could. So I think I've always given lots of space to build community and ground ourselves and connect any time we're together, but I think extra attention and extra time to allow them to just kind of talk about where they were, and just bring that into the space and give them voice and just allow them to just be exhausted together.

Another participant drew boundaries because class extended late into the evenings, and she had often been working since early in the morning, but she would plan to meet with and follow up with students. Participants consistently described using students' preferred communication methods, ensuring that the individual student preferences of communication (Noddings, 2012) were met, specifically identifying these as text, Zoom, phone, and/or email.

"Flexibility" was frequently mentioned regarding social emotional learning and trauma-informed teaching. One participant said, "For me, and probably a lot of people who have given grace to yourself and my students actually. . . . The grace that you expect collective, communal grace." The participants focused particularly on being flexible with due dates; considered personal and family health concerns; and did not require camera use. One participant pointed to specific situations where leadership education students struggled to meet requirements for internships, and the instructor and her colleagues found ways to be flexible with students (Noddings, 2005, 2012). "I know lots of times this year they wouldn't have planning periods. They might have to cover because they can't get enough subs . . . to provide class coverage." Without the planning period, the students would not have opportunities to conduct observations and engage in internship opportunities.

Some of the participants taught in programs that were currently online programs, so adjusting curriculum and pedagogy to an online context was not a challenge. However, for other participants, being online and being isolated from students were difficult for them as professionals and as people.

> I resisted online learning because . . . I want to see my students and I want to be with them. . . . The pandemic caused me to no longer resist that. I had to do it. And so, I had to jump in fully. It was messy at first, and I would tell them [the students] that I'm a new learner, but here's my reason why. I led with the why I wanted to do it [the reason behind the lesson], so they would understand.

Another participant described his ability to adapt to the online environment, which helped him provide learning and a supportive environment for students. "As I became more proficient with Zoom and using breakout rooms, they still were able to have their discussions." Moreover, he noted benefits from synchronous video conferencing. "And this may sound weird, but I feel like in some ways, especially some of the males, they were more transparent on Zoom than they would have been maybe in the same room looking at each of us eye to eye."

Participants repeatedly discussed the purpose of the creation of these caring environments, which was to facilitate effective leadership learning that would lead to better environments and student success at the education institutions where these educational leadership teachers' students worked. For example, one participant said that she worked to facilitate a safe and caring classroom space online,

> because I care about the children that they are serving and the families that they are serving, and I want those kids and those parents to be able to realize their dreams and see their potential. And they won't be able to do that if they don't have a leadership team that is creating those same spaces that I want to create in my class.

Developing Caring Relationships

Creating caring spaces was related to participants' developing caring relationships with students. One participant emphasized the importance of relationships that would ultimately lead the instructor to be able to better relate relevance and encourage rigor in teaching and learning.

> So, "rigor, relevance, and relationship" was a big catchphrase a few years ago. I think it's backwards; I think it should be "relationship, relevance, and rigor" and that you were able to get the rigor once the teachers, and once the students that you're dealing with know that you care and know that you're really in there right next to them working.

There was a sense of relationships being central to being able to reach and teach students during this time. Like Noddings's (2012) description of the reciprocal ethics of care, one participant described developing relationships so that she and her students are "going to be able to learn and grow together, and . . . I share with the students that I learned from them, just as much as I hope that they learned from me."

Communication became particularly important in developing these relationships. Participants named texting and Zoom as primary means of communication for building relationships with students. One participant reported that students would come to him, saying, "'Hey, I'm having this issue at work. Do you mind if we just chat about it over text?' And . . . we did." Recognizing the importance of relationship-building not only for teaching and learning and connecting during a stressful time, participants also reported that modeling relationship-building and face-to-face interactions were important in helping students to learn how to interact with others in their future careers. For example, one participant used Zoom and face-to-face options frequently because "you got to be able to read people's faces when you're dealing with upset parents or concerned teachers; that's huge for the administrators."

The participants consistently remarked that they made interactions with students a priority, providing a heightened responsiveness and a heightened awareness of building empathy and communicating that empathy.

> And they knew they could count on me. And so, in a time of unpredictability and uncertainty, it was nice to know they could count on me. And for that part of their life, and it wasn't just . . . college life, it was also their personal, and I mean I truly became a support coach for them.

They integrated check-ins for relationship-building and attempted to respond to students as quickly as possible. Noddings (2012) underscored the importance of listening "emotionally as well as intellectually" (p. 774) and sometimes setting aside subject matter to build relationships and trust that will ultimately assist the educator in reaching the student academically.

Achieving Learning Objectives and Adapting

Participants frequently emphasized that while they "adapted," they did not compromise "quality," "integrity," "expectations," or "rigor." Participants engaged in quality checks to ensure that objectives were met and students were performing well and passing licensure exams. Participants thought it part of their moral and ethical duties to hold students to high expectations and to prepare them for the realities of educational leadership positions, and several participants connected having high expectations for students with the need for them to develop core leadership competencies to support teachers' work and students' successful learning.

> We could not afford to lower expectations because then we would cheat them of what they rightfully deserved and paid for and are striving for.
>
> It's to care enough about them that I want them when they leave my class to be better for their kids [at their schools].
>
> I would say, still holding high expectations [is important] . . . because you know we don't want these teachers thinking it's okay not to have good RTI [Response to Intervention], not to have PLCs [Professional Learning Communities] looking at data.
>
> It's "adjust" expectations but don't lower them.

Participants pointed specifically to adapting to provide more trauma-informed pedagogy, curriculum, and instruction. They related this to the traumatic experiences they were undergoing during this time. Participants reported students' spouses and family members getting COVID-19, and some died. Participants themselves, their families, and their students also became ill with COVID-19. One participant reported that isolation was "like the cruelest thing you can do to anybody." Participants integrated reflection exercises into the curriculum to tie their leadership learning to their contexts and what they were dealing with in their lives. One participant reported using "collaborative conversations, and . . . these students . . . challenge you. . . . When I work with students, I want them to be really reflective because . . . learning doesn't happen just from what you learned, but also [from] reflecting on what you learn." Several participants underscored the importance of contextual learning during the pandemic, with one saying: "I also want you to integrate that into . . . your current context, so I want you to be able to construct meaning from what we're learning in a way that supports you in your current context." Noddings (2012) and Dewey (1963) contended that educative experiences link past, current, and future educational experiences to current life experiences. Similarly, these educators focused on using the pandemic and students' experiences as "teachable moments," whereby the students reflected on their experiences and their coursework learning and integrated those into future leadership practices.

Wellness and Mental Health

Mental health and wellness were threads throughout participants' narratives, both for themselves and their families, as well as for students. As one participant asserted, "I think the most valuable lesson during this whole time as a professor, is that it's wellness." Several participants mentioned allowing students to have cameras off and being thoughtful about backgrounds. Another participant reported the intentional teaching and modeling of social emotional learning, influenced by Angela Duckworth and Carol Dweck. All participants reported roles as caregivers and mental health supporters for students.

> We had to be the anchor and the stability and the comfort, the safe haven for any student, and so that's what we had to become . . . but we really truly had this pandemic and the world was falling apart around us, the pressure, stress, but we had to keep going. And we put that smile on our faces.

However, participants reported self-care challenges due to caring for others (students, faculty, staff, as well as their own families). For some participants who were used to teaching face-to-face, self-care was a challenge because they could not have the same interaction with their students and others in person, demonstrating the relational aspect of how caring for self is caring for others, and caring for others is caring for self (Noddings, 2005). One participant offered the following: "And so I think that's the other side of the story that we need to kind of explore more when we're thinking about COVID. Yes, there were a lot of resources for students. But what about the people who are actually taking care of the students and how they are being supported at that time?" Another participant commented on the many challenges related to working from home during the pandemic. "All of my children and my husband were now in the house as well. So, I went from me working in the home, doing what I needed to do on my own to now we have six people in the house, learning online and then my husband working and taking meetings and me doing that as well." As Conroy (2019) and Pignatelli (2015) have contended, educational leaders need to develop self-care strategies to maximize their wellness and their leadership performance.

Many participants reported doing what many people did during the pandemic to care for themselves. For example, they reported doing the following: exercising, meditating, spending time outdoors, reading for pleasure, spending time with immediate family members in their households, and completing home-improvement projects. Another participant cooked food for family members and would drop it off at their doors. Participants met with family members on Zoom and even played games on Zoom.

Discussion

The existing literature (including, for example, studies by Berkovich and Eyal [2020] and Gerstl-Pepin et al. [2006]), reveals deficiencies in educational leadership programs' approaches to teaching ethics—in particular, ethical leadership and social justice theories and practices. Gerstl-Pepin and collaborators (2006) recommended that educational leadership programs more intentionally integrate ethics and social justice education within the programs' curricula. We have extended these findings since our participants reported integrating ethics of care into their curricula and pedagogies and achieving success with students through this integration. Bryson (2021), a social work educator, and Persky (2021), an educational leadership teacher, reflected on their personal approaches to demonstrating the ethics of care. As our findings also demonstrated, Persky shared that, during the pandemic, her priority was shifting the modality of the class for the students without affecting the rigor or engagement aspects of the course. Much like our participants, Bryson described her approach as a social work educator and administrator to demonstrate the ethics of care; she described the trauma of the pandemic where some students needed to turn off cameras while others left cameras on with children, pets, family members cooking, and even people commuting in their cars in the background. As our participants did, she "invited people to just be in the space, however they were, no matter what their houses and lives looked like" (p. 633). Bryson's reflection provides some applicable insights for our study, yet it is limited to this one program's and one administrator's dedication to "rejecting indifference" during the pandemic. Likewise, Corbera and fellow researchers (2020) discussed the need for educational leadership instructors to refocus on often-overlooked aspects of the profession and to pay more attention to the diverse and at times conflicting emotions and life experiences of our students. Our results address the gaps in the literature about educational leadership faculties' development of important caring strategies that assisted their teaching and student learning during the COVID-19 pandemic; these educators' ethics of care have implications for forming ethical and caring educational leaders. Specifically, this study addresses the gaps in the literature about the ways in which educational leadership faculty have integrated ethics of care into their curriculum, modeled caring and trauma-informed pedagogy, held students to high expectations while maintaining flexibility, and navigated the pandemic both personally and professionally.

Implications for Research

We have identified multiple possibilities for future research. For example, researchers could further study students' perceptions of educational leadership professionals teaching during the pandemic, using quantitative, qualitative, or mixed-methods approaches. More generalizable results could be derived from conducting a quantitative study and using survey instruments for educational leadership students and educators in order to learn more about teaching and learning experiences, both pre-pandemic and during the pandemic. Because participants consistently discussed "adjusting" without compromising their constructs of rigor and high expectations, further study of the strategies that educators used is necessary. Another thread throughout the narratives was trauma-informed teaching and learning; therefore, there are opportunities for further study of socio-emotional and trauma-informed teaching and learning practices in educational leadership programs.

Implications for Practice

Related to many of the implications for research are many of the implications for practice. For example, departments can provide training for educational leadership instructors on providing flexibility while maintaining rigor, specifically defining "rigor" and strategies for maintaining it, as well as defining "flexibility" and associated strategies. Other training and professional development opportunities for educational leadership and other educators include workshops and sessions on socio-emotional learning and trauma-informed care for educational leadership professionals. Educational leadership departments have opportunities to develop professional learning communities (PLCs) for educational leadership instructors to share learning, to assess programs, and to support one another with self-care.

Overall, participants mentioned that some universities and departments provided resources and support for faculty and students during challenging times better than other departments and universities did. However, several participants mentioned that there was greater focus on care for students than care for faculty and staff during the pandemic. PK–12 schools, colleges, and universities have opportunities to provide greater levels of support during challenging times such as academic support provided through multiple modalities and counseling for students, faculty, staff, and administrators.

Conclusions

The COVID-19 pandemic created an actuality where loss and change were constant. And even in this state of flux and uncertainty, people were resilient in their attempts to construct a reality as close to "normal" as they could. This is also true of educational leadership professionals, who practiced the ethic of care through demonstrations of flexibility in pedagogy and modality. Participants were able to balance flexibility and caring with their commitment to student learning, while also taking steps to engage in self-care during the COVID-19 pandemic. Additionally, our participants were acutely aware that educational leadership students must be held to rigorous standards so that they can meet course learning outcomes, pass licensure exams, and effectively serve students, parents, teachers, and communities within their own contexts.

References

Anderson, R. C., Bousselot, T., Katz-Buoincontro, J., & Todd, J. (2021). Generating buoyancy in a sea of uncertainty: Teachers' creativity and well-being during the COVID-19 pandemic. *Frontiers in Psychology, 11*. https://doi.org/10.3389/fpsyg.2020.614774

Bergmark, U. (2020). Teachers' professional learning when building a research-based education: Context-specific, collaborative and teacher-driven professional development. *Professional Development in Education*, pp. 1–15. https://doi.org.proxy.mau.se/10.1080/19415257.2020.1827011

Berkovich, I. (2017). Reflections on leadership preparation programs and social justice: Are the power and the responsibility of the faculty all in the design? *Journal of Educational Administration, 55*(3), 261–279.

Berkovich, I., & Eyal, O. (2020). School leaders' emotional support of teachers through emotional transformation: Qualitative insights into the maintenance of teachers' occupational identity. *Leadership and Policy in Schools, 19*(4), 625–639.

Berry, B. (2020). Teaching, learning, and caring in the post-COVID era. *Phi Delta Kappan, 102*(1), 14–17. https://doi.org/10.1177/0031721720956840

Brown, K. M. (2004). Leadership for social justice and equity: Weaving a transformative framework and pedagogy. *Educational Administration Quarterly, 40*(1), 77–108.

Bryson, S. A. (2021). An ethic of care? Academic administration and pandemic policy. *Qualitative Social Work, 20*(1–2), 632–638. https://doi.org/10.1177/1473325020973386

Cambron-McCabe, N., & McCarthy, M. M. (2005). Educating school leaders for social justice. *Educational Policy, 19*(1), 201–222.

Capper, C. A., Theoharis, G., & Sebastian, J. (2006). Toward a framework for preparing leaders for social justice. *Journal of Educational Administration, 44*(3), 209–224.

Conroy, T. J. (2019). *Sketching the ethic of care in educational leadership: Portraits of four authentic leaders.* (Publication No. 13898623.) [Doctoral Dissertation, Cabrini University]. ProQuest Dissertations and Theses Global.

Corbera, E., Anguelovski, I., Honey-Rosés, J., & Ruiz-Mallén, I. (2020). Academia in the time of COVID-19: Towards an ethics of care. *Planning Theory & Practice, 21*(2), 191–199. http://doi.org/10.1080/14649357.2020.1757891

Creswell, J. W., & Creswell, J. D. (2018). *Research design: Qualitative, quantitative, and mixed methods* (5th ed.). SAGE.

DeMartino, L. (2021). Adult learners, remote learning, and the COVID pandemic: Restructuring education doctorate courses in crisis. *Impacting Education: Journal on Transforming Professional Practice, 6*(2), 11–15. https://doi.org/10.5195/ie.2021.160

Dewey, J. (1963 [1938]). *Experience and education.* Macmillan.

Durlak, J. A., Weissberg, R. P., Dymnicki, A. B., Taylor, R. D., & Schellinger, K. B. (2011). The impact of enhancing students' social and emotional learning: A meta-analysis of school-based universal interventions. *Child Development, 82*(1), 405–432. https://doi.org/10.1111/j.1467-8624.2010.01564.x

Eadie, P., Levickis, P., Murray, L., Page, J., Elek, C., & Church, A. (2021). Early childhood educators' wellbeing during the COVID-19 pandemic. *Early Childhood Education Journal, 49*(5), 903–913. https://doi.org/10.1007/s10643-021-01203-3

Elias, M. J., & Weissberg, R. P. (2000). Primary prevention: Educational approaches to enhance social and emotional learning. *Journal of School Health, 70*(5), 186–190. https://doi.org/10.1111/j.1746-1561.2000.tb06470.x

Eveleigh, A., Cook, A., Naples, L. H., & Cipriano, C. (2022). How did educators of students with learning differences use social–emotional learning to support their students and themselves early in the COVID-19 pandemic? *Children & Schools, 44*(1), 27–38. https://doi.org/10.1093/cs/cdab030

Furman, G. (2012). Social justice leadership as praxis: Developing capacities through preparation programs. *Educational Administration Quarterly, 48*,(2),191–229.

Gerstl-Pepin, C., Killeen, K., and Hasazi, S. (2006). Utilizing an "ethic of care" in leadership preparation: Uncovering the complexity of colorblind social justice. *Journal of Educational Administration, 44*(3), 250–263. https://doi.org/10.1108/09578230610664841

Gilligan, C. J. (1982). *In a different voice*. Harvard University Press.

Goldstein, L. S. (1998). More than gentle smiles and warm hugs: Applying the ethic of care to early childhood education. *Journal of Research in Childhood Education, 12*(2), 244–261. https://doi.org/10.1080/02568549809594888

Häggström, F., Borsch, A. S., & Skovdal, M. (2020). Caring alone: The boundaries of teachers' ethics of care for newly arrived immigrant and refugee learners in Denmark. *Children and Youth Services Review, 117*. https://doi.org/10.1016/j.childyouth.2020.105248

Hawk, T. F. (2017). Getting to know your students and an educational ethic of care. *Journal of Management Education, 41*(5), 669–686. https://doi.org/10.1177/1052562917716488

Held, V. (2006). *The ethics of care: Personal, political, and global*. Oxford University Press.

Hoyt, L. T., Cohen, A. K., Dull, B., Maker Castro, E., & Yazdani, N. (2021). "Constant stress has become the new normal": Stress and anxiety inequalities among U.S. college students in the time of COVID-19. *Journal of Adolescent Health, 68*(2), 270–276. https://doi.org/10.1016/j.jadohealth.2020.10.030

Johnston, O., Wildy, H., & Shand, J. (2022). "That teacher really likes me"—Student-teacher interactions that initiate teacher expectation effects by developing caring relationships. *Learning and Instruction*. Volume 80. https://doi.org/10.1016/j.learninstruc.2022.101580

Liu, B. F., Shi, D., Lim, J. R., Islam, K., Edwards, A. L., & Seeger, M. (2021). When crises hit home: How U.S. higher education leaders navigate values during uncertain times. *Journal of Business Ethics, 179*, 353–368 https://doi.org/10.1007/s10551-021-04820-5

Madrigal, L., & Blevins, A. (2021). "I hate it, it's ruining my life": College students' early academic year experiences during the COVID-19 pandemic. *Traumatology, 28*(3), 325–335 https://doi.org/10.1037/trm0000336

McClellan, R., & Dominguez, R. (2006). The uneven march toward social justice: Diversity, conflict, and complexity in educational administration programs. *Journal of Educational Administration, 40*(3), 225–238.

McKenzie, K. B., Christman, D. E., Hernandez, F., Fierro, E., Capper, C. A., Dantley, M., Gonzalez, M. L., Cambron-McCabe, N., & Scheurich, J. J. (2008). From the field: A proposal for educating leaders for social justice. *Educational Administration Quarterly, 44*(1), 111–138.

Moustakas, C. (1994). *Phenomenological research methods*. SAGE.

Noddings, N. (1984). *Caring: A feminine approach to ethics and moral education*. University of California Press.

Noddings, N. (1992). *The challenge to care in schools*. Teachers College Press.

Noddings, N. (2005). *The challenge to care in schools: An alternative approach to education*. Teachers College Press.

Noddings, N. (2010). Moral education in an age of globalization. *Educational Philosophy and Theory, 42*(4), 390–396. http://doi: 10.1111/j.1469-5812.2008.00487.x

Noddings, N. (2012). The caring relation in teaching. *Oxford Review of Education, 38*(6), 771–781. https://doi.org/10.1080/03054985.2012.745047

Noddings, N. (2013). *Education and democracy in the 21st century*. Teachers College Press.

Page, J. (2018). Characterising the principles of professional love in early childhood care and education. *International Journal of Early Years Education, 26*(2), 125–141. https://doi.org/10.1080/09669760.2018.1459508

Persky, J. (2021). Higher education and the ethic of care: Finding a way forward during a global pandemic. *Cultural Studies ↔ Critical Methodologies, 21*(3), 301–305. https://doi.org/10.1177/15327086211002776

Pignatelli, F. (2015). Ethical leadership development as care of the self: A Foucauldian perspective. *Schools: Studies in Education, 12*(2), 198–213.

Primdahl, N. L., Borsch, A. S., Verelst, A., Jervelund, S. S., Derluyn, I., & Skovdal, M. (2020). "It's difficult to help them when I am not sitting next to them": How COVID-19 school closures interrupted teachers' care for newly arrived migrant and refugee learners in Denmark. *Vulnerable Children and Youth Studies*. https://doi.org/10.1080/17450128.2020.1829228

Rabin, C., & Smith, G. (2016). "My lesson plan was perfect until I tried to teach": Care ethics into practice in classroom management. *Journal of Research in Childhood Education, 30*(4), 600–617. https://doi.org/10.1080/02568543.2016.1214192

Riemen, D. J. (1986). The essential structure of a caring interaction: Doing phenomenology. In P. M. Munhall & C. J. Oiler (Eds.), *Nursing research: A qualitative perspective* (pp. 85–105). Appleton & Lange.

Sleeter, C. (1996). *Multicultural education as social activism*. State University of New York Press.

Soncini, A., Politi, E., & Matteucci, M. C. (2021). Teachers navigating distance learning during COVID-19 without feeling emotionally exhausted: The protective role of self-efficacy. *School Psychology, 36*(6), 494–503. http://dx.doi.org/10.1037/spq0000469

Sorrells, C., & Madrid Akpovo, S. (2022). "You can hold two things to be true at the same time": Duality in ECE teachers' emotional experiences during COVID-19. *Journal of Research in Childhood Education*. 36:4, 663–680, https://doi.org/10.1080/02568543.2022.2044415

Valicenti-McDermott, M., O'Neil, M., Morales-Lara, A., Seijo, R., Fried, T., & Shulman, L. (2022). Remote learning experience for children with developmental disabilities during COVID-19 pandemic in an ethnically diverse community. *Journal of Child Neurology, 37*, 50–55. 10.1177/08830738211040296

Varga, M. A., & Paulus, T. (2014). Grieving online: Newcomers' constructions of grief in an online support group. *Death Studies, 38*, 443–449. https://doi.org/10.1080/07481187.2013.780112

Yang, C. (2021). Online teaching self-efficacy, social–emotional learning (SEL) competencies, and compassion fatigue among educators during the COVID-19 pandemic. *School Psychology Review, 50*(4), 505–518. https://doi.org/10.1080/2372966X.2021.1903815

Zieher, A. K., Cipriano, C., Meyer, J. L., & Strambler, M. J. (2021). Educators' implementation and use of social and emotional learning early in the COVID-19 pandemic. *School Psychology, 36*(5), 388–397. https://doi.org/10.1037/spq0000461.supp (Supplemental)

THREE

Viral Epistolary: A Digital Community for Individual and Collective Writing at the Time of the First COVID-19 Wave

Ciro De Vincenzo, Anita Franceschi, and Monica Massari

Introduction

The COVID-19 pandemic emerged in 2020 as a phenomenon that disrupted our taken-for-granted daily life, plunging into crisis our collective as well as individual identities (Demertzis & Eyerman, 2020; Matthewman & Huppatz, 2020) while enhancing, especially during the recurrent lockdown measures adopted by most countries, the emergence of new social rhythms in everyday life and activities (Alexander & Smith, 2020; Erll, 2020). In a world where physical closeness and in-person proximity were forbidden, new modes of experiencing community emerged (Cocorullo et al., 2022). Millions of people around the globe, suddenly confined to their homes, increasingly turned to digital and social media not only for the purpose of receiving information about the spread of the virus, but also for setting up new forms of communication with others that could facilitate a sense of sharing of their experiences, beliefs, expectations, and fears (Bolander & Smith, 2020; Thorndahl & Frandsen, 2020). Moreover, a widespread need to re-think the relationship between the self and the other emerged, as well as to make sense of the crisis that COVID-19 created at many levels and to find a way in the struggle with the enhanced reflexivity engendered by the pandemic (Markham, Harris, & Luka, 2020). Most important, an urgent need to share intimate stories of lived experiences of that extraordinary moment emerged, together with a wide range of emotionally charged narratives. The latter have come to represent a wealth of sources that are already being widely used in an attempt to encode our experience and memory for future reference (Adams & Kopelman, 2022; Erll, 2020).

This chapter examines a case study referring to a collective writing project called "Viral Epistolary" (VE) that was launched through a website and social media accounts (i.e., Facebook and Instagram) during the initial wave of the COVID-19 pandemic in the context of the first Italian lockdown (from March to June 2020). VE's aim was to create an online meeting-point for sharing feelings and views related to domestic isolation, physical distancing, and quarantine pandemic experiences by using the epistolary genre as a mediation, meaning-making, and autobiographical tool. In particular, the core project was aimed at creating a digital space for sharing experiences through anonymous digital letter-writing that could solicit replies from a wider online community. Although not originally conceived as part of a research project, VE ended up providing such a rich and stimulating wealth of materials (letters, posts, and drawings) that the team involved in this initiative later decided to reconceive the aims and scope of the project. After all of the participants were informed of the project and asked to provide their consent, an attempt was made to analyze the outcome of the first three months of the project within a wider theoretical and epistemological framework while maintaining an awareness of the risks and limits implied in any attempt to observe a phenomenon while it is still ongoing. Thus, this chapter provides an analysis of a specific phase of VE's experience—i.e., the initial one coinciding with the most obscure and heterogeneous expectations about such an unknown phenomenon (a global pandemic affecting humans)—since Italy was among the western countries that immediately adopted, in March 2020, the most comprehensive lockdown measures.

The first section herein provides information on the methodology adopted throughout the project, while the ensuing sections contain descriptions of the case and an analysis of the main outcomes that emerged. The final part is devoted to concluding remarks.

Methodology: Writing as an Ethical, Epistemological, and Methodological Site

The narratives used in the analysis are part of the letters written and shared by VE's participants, who animated the first three months of the project. They were invited to address feelings, experiences, and meanings associated with the pandemic scenario from a subjective perspective and to incorporate them into letters as a form of self-reflection. The overall idea driving the project was to enhance autobiographical writing that, being online, could potentially involve a wide and heterogeneous audience willing to engage in the same collective exercise (Stanley, 2004; 2015). Thus, the implicit pact agreed to by participants required compliance infused with a certain degree of authenticity.

The decision to begin a research project inspired by this initiative, however, came later, since the letters we received immediately revealed a rich field of autobiographical insight shedding light on wider social and historical practices that could provide a fertile source and a tool for enhancing sociological imagination (Plummer, 2001; Tamboukou, 2011; 2020). Consequently—and bearing in mind that the letters received and shared throughout the project should be considered as fragments of lived experiences—they nevertheless reveal multiple layers of meaning (Haggis & Holmes, 2011; Jolly, 1999). This raises questions regarding many complex issues, including subjectivity, identity, truth, power, representations, and desires, to name but a few, that require a methodological and epistemological sensitivity (Butler, 2017; Tamboukou, 2020).

In the framework of this analysis, VE's letters are considered, on the one hand, as narratives that expressly aim at enhancing channels of communication between the authors and any reader, offering rich insights into shared experience of the pandemic, and, on the other, as expressions of that epistolary "technology of self" that intervenes "in the constitution of the social and the subject herself" (Tambouku, 2011, p. 627).

In order to make VE available to everyone who wished to take part in or be involved with the project, a website, along with Facebook and Instagram accounts, was created that allowed people to join the community by entering their personal email address in a dedicated section. The website also aimed at providing information about the project to those who decided to write a letter and/or to start a correspondence to share their experiences. Finally, ten tips were provided to potential writers: be simple, try to refer to details, write the letter as a gift, be kind, take all the time needed, ask questions, help those who are in need, use not only words but also sounds and paintings, enjoy it, and re-read it if you would like to.

Case Analysis

During the three-month project, which lasted from the very first day of the national lockdown measures to their official end, a letter was forwarded daily to all 332 people who had subscribed to the website. However, people could participate in the project and interact with the community either by writing a "prompt" letter or replying to one specific letter—a "correspondence" letter—and, in this way, begin a correspondence with the original writer. Replies to the letter were not limited in terms of length or number, and the initial writer could choose whether or not to reply. All the letters collected during the project were made available on the website, allowing users to read both the letters and the replies, and to write a new letter by hitting the designated key. Finally, people could also decide not to write letters and to simply enjoy reading all or part of others' correspondence. Figure 1 shows the workflow of the project.

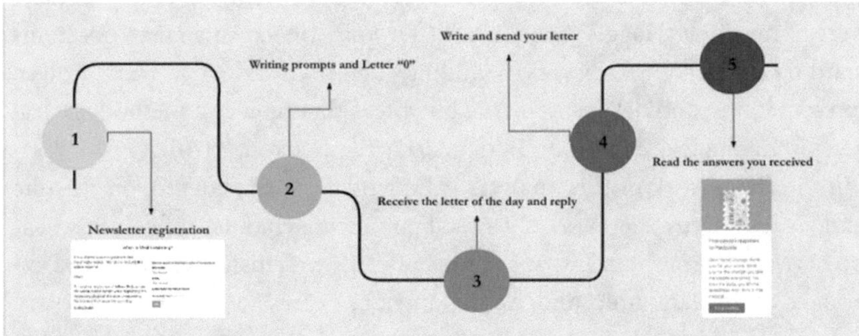

Figure 3.1. Workflow to write, receive, and reply to a letter.

Overall, 332 people subscribed to VE, and the project collected 340 letters including the replies. Of the 332 people who subscribed, 172 wrote a letter, while the remaining 160 participated by reading the letters that were sent daily. Overall, 85 were first letters ("prompt letters"), that is, spontaneously written letters by one of the project's participants, while the remaining 255 were letters written in reply ("correspondence letters").

In order to enrich and valorise the experience of subscribing to VE, artists and cartoonists from all over Italy were involved in the project. Each of the 85 prompt letters was accompanied by an illustration based on the content addressed in the letter itself. All illustrations produced were made openly accessible on VE's social media.[1]

The first letter was delivered on 27 March 2020 and the last one on 13 June of the same year. Letters written and shared during the project were mostly from Italy, but others were also from France, Spain, and England. All letters were written in Italian, since all the authors had a good mastery of the language. This made it possible to avoid translating them, thus avoiding the risk of altering their original meaning.

Before presenting and discussing some preliminary results of this project, a few more words about the genesis and the starting group of VE are in order. Indeed, the very first idea of creating a digital space where people could share their experiences in a friendly and informal environment came from F., an early-career, female Italian psychologist and psychotherapist. As the first public health measures were adopted, she thought that having a place of engagement developed within a writing community supported by digital social media would be an effective tool to: (a) encourage reflection on the social dimension of health by creating a "circular" space where people could share their feelings; (b) promote a civic commitment with respect to the management of our own and others' health; and (c) create a virtual space where social interactions could be still maintained and cultivated, with a view toward enhancing mutual exchange and support. As soon as she proposed that idea, she connected with C., a male PhD student in the social sciences, and R., a female sales consultant, in order to develop her idea through a dedicated website, as well as Facebook and Instagram accounts. Once the technical and basic structural aspects of the project were developed, the group grew bigger by welcoming six other people, including A., a male Italian archaeologist living in France and teaching at a school there; V., a female Italian architect; and Ch., a male specializing in social start-ups; and, finally, three other early-career, female Italian psychologists: A., G., and B.

"I Truly Understood We Are Grains of Sand": Revelations and Relations at the Time of the First COVID-19 Wave

As reported above, the entire corpus of data consisted of 340 letters (85 "prompt letters" and 225 "correspondence letters") written by 172 unique writers. On top of that, 85 drawings made by emerging Italian artists and representing the basic content and meaning of the prompt letters completed the data set. Therefore, the richness (the average length of letters was one and one-half pages) and density (in terms of content, since many letters referred to one another in an ongoing, asynchronous correspondence) of the materials gathered, as well as the different dimensions and levels through which an analysis of textual data can be performed, have already inspired several works.[2] However, little attention has been paid thus far to two other issues addressed earlier in this chapter.

First, the initial COVID-19 wave (and its consequent domestic isolation, physical distancing, and forced quarantining—all harsh public health measures) as a critical event can be addressed along a destructive "revelation" timeframe: "something" was torn apart, and "something else" was discovered.[3] As the pandemic unfolded by (provisionally or not) erasing everyday structural and contextual forms of socio-psychological organization, it simultaneously offered an opportunity to both symbolically and practically interact, reflect, and realize an insight into what comprised the essential ground of one's personal and social life. In and through the "meanwhile" of the pandemic—a time of transition in which to feel the effects of the tension between experience and expectation, as suggested by the concept of "horizon" (Pickering, 2004)—perceived and constructed as a sociohistorical event whose temporality is stretched and ubiquitous rather than perfunctory (Wagner-Pacifici, 2010), something happened in the deepest recesses of ourselves. Writing became more than an act of mutual exchange of information (a "commercial" dimension of every relationship); it evolved into a form of intimate confession that helped to anchor "realizations/revelations," thus transforming COVID-19 from a critical societal event to a proper collective, compressed trauma (Demertzis & Eyerman, 2020; Masiero et al., 2020). In other words, there was a *moment* of truly felt awareness in the *time* of COVID-19. The first pandemic wave constituted a liminal experience working as a general symbolic resource (Salvatore et al., 2019) through which all the "unframed" societal and personal experiences could be explained, both in affective—that is, in terms of our private and intimate dimension—and rhetorical ways—in other words, referring to the social construction of reality.[4]

Second, as harsh public health measures were adopted, consolidated forms of social relations, everyday (often empty) interactional and communicative rituals (such as asking "How is it going?" or "What's new?") acquired a deeper sense of concern toward others' well-being. Whether an individual was suffering or not, and independent of the actual personal experiential elaboration of the pandemic, the collective atmosphere of grief and fear (Tateo et al., 2022) brought by it required a relational space-time of caring to be developed, wherein tolerance and compassion could be expressed without limits, thus allowing a reconciliation (even if temporary) with an imagined "Italian suffering community" (Anderson, 1983).

Revelations and Relationships: Unintentional Consequences of the Pandemic

We would like to begin the presentation of our case study with a "correspondence letter." L. is replying to F., who was relating her anxieties about the current situation and, most importantly, about the future. She admitted that, in having to deal with issues that she was not familiar with, she had never experienced such a difficult time. She discovered a new, unexplored dimension and asked the community how to deal with it. As L. says, COVID-19 is a "*fruitful time to name them* [the deepest anxieties]." However, this difficult personal task is just a step: Nothing ends with it, as "[COVID-19] *causes my mind to go beyond my individuality*."

> Hi F., I found your letter two days later. . . . While I was reading it, I immediately had the desire to reply you. I believe that this time of dilation that we must live through has a consequence: the emergence of our deepest anxieties. It is a fruitful time to name them. It has happened to me in the past, and surprisingly now my personal anguish has a more subdued voice; I am almost surprised by this, but I think this is mainly due to two reasons. Firstly, because for years I have given them space, by now I know them, by now I have learned to master them; now, after so long, I am trying to reconcile with my demons. Secondly, I think that the period we are living in, with deaths all around us and the collective grief that comes with it, *causes my mind to go beyond my individuality and be more dismayed at this unprecedented view of our world.*

The next letter, a "prompt" one, is written by D. Throughout the letter, she wonders about what she is learning from the pandemic. She first looks back at what she has lost, and all of the habits that she has had to change. Soon after, she questions whether there is something that can be saved. With the help of pressing and evocative prose, she shares that she "*appreciated happiness on a rainy day . . . rediscovered a passion for tiny things . . . discovered the allure of waking up early in the morning for a hike.*" As for L., such realizations and revelations do not occur in an empty or inaccessible space; rather, they are triggered by relationships, which bring us "outside" to a partially known/unknown space in which self-reflection and inner exploration are possible.

> May this be a flowery time? I wonder if there are times without flowers. In this time of lockdown—what an unromantic word—I have tried to learn to sustain the beauty of life. I admit that I have not always succeeded. I have found my morning prayer in dew. I met my faith in a blooming cactus flower. I have appreciated happiness on a rainy day by photographing the drops of water on tulip petals. I rediscovered a passion for tiny things: those that no one ever pays attention to; those that escape the unobservant eye; those that are hidden; a tiny strawberry well hidden in the undergrowth; a tiny spider clinging to a leaf. I discovered the allure of waking up early in the morning for a hike around the corner. I tried to pause with my mind and body, but mostly with my eyes. I want to share with you what nature has taught me and teaches me every day: beauty can always find a space in which to flourish. You just have to know how to look. With affection, a close though distant reader.

From a literary point of view, M.'s letter, like the previous one, is beautiful. Her writing is pressing, enthusiastic, and constantly oscillating between different feelings. Words seem to flow as in a river, one after the other, like a pianist playing the piano in an urgent, rhythmic way. It is a letter full of interesting clues: the *I* and the *we* are constantly alternating around the theme of discoveries and awakenings ("*I actually find that I should dance a little more . . . we will find ourselves appreciating and understanding some important individual freedoms . . . I recognized, after a few weeks, how physiological the alternation of these feelings is*"), since the pandemic is perceived as a unique time for everybody ("*I hope we will all come out stronger . . . that many can take this opportunity to look inside themselves, identifying and analyzing their priorities . . . A navigation within the self that few times we have time to investigate*"). What captured our attention in M.'s letter is also—in regard to the topic of relationships—the "*hope for a we*," not just for one's self and, as in the previous letter, the "*tolerance*" such moments of grief can teach, by introducing a novel perspective in one's everyday life.

> I've been living away from them for years, and with a few notes of Didi by Khaled, I'm dancing alone in my small room, as if the three of them are in front of me and we're all moving together in time to the music. This amuses me a lot, and a little trick that I have found activates a good dose of good humour in me right away. I actually find that I should dance a little more. Movement and fun. Do you find yourself dancing alone in the house? In the kitchen while preparing something? After a glass of wine at the end of the day? I agree when you write

> that we will find ourselves appreciating and understanding some important individual freedoms at the end of this intense quarantine period. I hope we will all come out stronger and more aware, I hope that many can take this opportunity to look inside themselves, identifying and analysing their priorities, their needs in social, affective, practical forms. A navigation within the self that we rarely have time to investigate. Personally, I feel that I put up, on a daily basis, a difficult self-control job. I try to rationalize the situation, the amount of information that comes to me and that I deliberately feed on, and I pose in a way that I would say it is almost "self-tolerant" toward the "no" moments that often surface, full of nervousness, anxiety, and worry. I recognized, after a few weeks, how physiological the alternation of these feelings is, how normal, how trivial.

The following is from R., replying to M., who was sharing how much he was feeling alone and how he missed his girlfriend—a completely new feeling for him, as he had always been a solitary person. R. alters the uneasiness into a transformative experience as he dares "*to think that it is because of this break that you have discovered that you love her.*" Again, a collective "we" is evoked and echoed in the form of an invitation to think "*beyond individuality*" and find a feeling of belonging, as well as relief in the collective condition.

> Dear M., I am writing you today, May 5, to share some very good news: the worst is over. We are no longer alone as we felt but it was right, in my opinion, to spend time just in company of ourselves. Should time stand still again, try not to experience the separation from the person you love badly, because I dare to think that it is because of this break that you have discovered that you love her.

The interdependence between a collective shared background and the context of novelty in societal and personal lives is also a prominent issue in D.'s reply to C., which invites us "*to look at ourselves, others, and society differently . . . some people have discovered themselves to be more fragile or stronger, what seemed to distance us has brought us together . . . we rediscover ourselves as people.*"

> Dear C., I think this situation is inviting us to look at ourselves, others, and society differently. Retirement homes have revealed themselves for what they are, poverty has exploded in all its evidence, some people have discovered themselves to be more fragile or stronger, what seemed to distance us has brought

us together, even creating complicity and intimacy. In silence, in slowness, in pain, we rediscover ourselves as people. Let us try not to waste this opportunity.

Concluding Remarks

The analysis of the outcomes of the first phase of our project, which was aimed at enhancing the launching of a digital community for individual and collective writing at the time of the first COVID-19 wave, suggests how letter writing is still a powerful form of intimate confession, one that actually enhances a reflection on the interdependencies that exist between personal and collective experiences, while fostering new expectational horizons. Moreover, the outcomes of the project emphasize a widely felt need to benefit from a space and time wherein mutual care, support, and compassion could be still expressed and, more crucially, further developed. As I. reports in the following letter:

> Dear Epistolary, now that the worst seems to be over, I am writing this letter to ask you not to forget. Tomorrow, when you return to your usual life, do not forget the suffering, the fear, the waiting of these still suspended days. But don't forget either the small daily joys and wonderful discoveries, the scent of a blossoming flower, the chirping of birds returning, announcing spring, the vivid colour of the sky and the sea, the life that goes on even (perhaps better) without us. Do not forget the delicacy of silence, nor the love in small gestures for and of the people you love. Try to remember all this, to appreciate more what you have in each and every moment. And maybe ask for less. From your loved ones, from yourself, from life. Don't forget that, after all, as you may have discovered these days, very little is needed to be happy. Value what is truly important and let go what is not. Do not chase dreams that do not belong to you. Don't compare yourself with others. Don't let ambition and desire corrode you. Find your purpose in life and, whatever it is, be proud of it. Live intensely, gratefully, and in harmony, since we have only one life. Be kind to yourself. Be patient with those you love. Don't get angry. Give thanks. Forgive. Do what makes you feel good, but do no harm. In fact, if you can, do something for others. Help an elderly person, give a smile to a stranger, save a stray, plant a tree. Don't forget that we are guests on this planet. The world exists and will continue to exist without us. Try to make it a better place or, at least, work to avoid making it a worse place. Make sure that your life has a plus sign in front of it, not a minus sign. Try to leave something good for those who come after. And, if at times life feels heavy, remember these days. It

is there that you will find the strength to keep walking, I am sure, in the right direction. Hugs to you.

She is writing at the end of the quarantine, when the Italian government announced the suspension of public health measures. Just a week, and all the people could be "free" again. But "free" from what, and especially what kind of "freedom"? Her letter seems to be an invitation to carefully reflect on the "*suspended days*" brought on by domestic isolation and physical distancing. A call for remembrance: "*not to forget*," when returning to your "*usual life*," the "*wonderful discoveries*," such as that "*very little is needed to be happy*."

The pandemic has provided a great social and collective opportunity to re-evaluate one's own priorities, to review—through new lenses—the multi-layered context of everyday life, and to rediscover "new" (or perhaps just usually underestimated) sources of mental health. In that sense, fragmented and shuttered communities have found themselves again at the intersection of a collective grief and hope, something that—at the beginning—was felt to be "democratic"[5]—a glue, making a supposed "us" together again, despite the fact that each one was physically apart.

Notes

1. https://www.facebook.com/epistolariovirale/ or https://www.instagram.com/epistolariovirale/

2. For the importance of writing in terms of "secret meaning," see Cocorullo and colleagues (2022), and for writing as a tool mediating between the material and transcendental nature of meaning, see De Vincenzo and fellow researchers (2022).

3. For a discussion of the resemblance to the concept of "liminality," see Stenner, 2017.

4. In using the word "rhetoric," we refer to the transformation of COVID-19 from an a-specific symbolic resource functioning as a liminal entity to a proper, discursive component working as a justifying platform, whether in the form of self-deceit (*in* the pandemic, as confirmed by the widespread use, at the time, of popular expressions such as "Everything will go well"), or in the form of a public framework ("*after* the pandemic"). In Italy, for example, the issue of "mental health"—historically not a central concept—has since been constantly anchored in the experience of the pandemic. In other words, this seems to emphasize the fact that "there will be a pre- and a post-" COVID-19 period.

5. Even though the virus is not democratic at all.

References

Adams, T., & Kopelman, S. (2022). Remembering COVID-19: Memory, crisis, and social media. *Media, Culture & Society, 44*(2), 266–285. https://doi.org/10.1177/01634437211048377

Alexander, J. C., & Smith, P. (2020). COVID-19 and symbolic action: Global pandemic as code, narrative, and cultural performance. *American Journal of Cultural Sociology, 8*(3), 263–269. https://doi.org/10.1057/s41290-020-00123-w

Anderson, B. (1983). *Imagined Communities: Reflections on the Origin and Spread of Nationalism.* Verso.

Bolander, B., & Smith, P. (2020). Time across the lines: Collaborative wonderings under COVID-19. *Qualitative Inquiry*, Sep; 27(7): 835–843. https://doi.org/10.1177/1077800420962476

Butler, S. E. (2017). Correspondence, peer support, and wellness: The influence of life writing on mental health. *a/b: Auto/Biography Studies, 32*(2), 404–406. https://doi.org/10.1080/08989575.2017.1289043

Cocorullo, A., Franceschi, A., Serio, F., & De Vincenzo, C. (2022). La «correspondance virale»: L'écriture comme thérapie en temps de confinement. In S. Ducas, R. De Angelis, & A. Cormier (Eds.), *Les Écritures Confinées*. Hermann.

De Vincenzo, C., Serio, F., Franceschi, A., Barbagallo, S., & Zamperini, A. (2022). A "viral epistolary" and psychosocial spirituality: Restoring transcendental meaning during COVID-19 through a digital community letter-writing project. *Pastoral Psychology.* https://doi.org/10.1007/s11089-021-00991-0

Demertzis, N., & Eyerman, R. (2020). COVID-19 as cultural trauma. *American Journal of Cultural Sociology, 8*(3), 428–450. https://doi.org/10.1057/s41290-020-00112-z

Erll, A. (2020). Afterword: Memory worlds in times of Corona. *Memory Studies, 13*(5), 861–874. https://doi.org/10.1177/1750698020943014

Haggis, J., & Holmes, M. (2011). Epistles to emails: Letters, relationship building and the virtual age. *Life Writing, 8*(2), 169–185. https://doi.org/10.1080/14484528.2011.559733

Jolly, M. (1999). Defining a field: The encyclopedia of life writing. *a/b: Auto/Biography Studies, 14*(2), 309–316. https://doi.org/10.1080/08989575.1999.10815225

Markham, A. N., Harris, A., & Luka, M. E. (2020). Massive and microscopic sensemaking during COVID-19 times. *Qualitative Inquiry, 27*(7). https://doi.org/10.1177/ 1077800420962477

Masiero, M., Mazzocco, K., Harnois, C., Cropley, M., & Pravettoni, G. (2020). From individual to social trauma: Sources of everyday trauma in Italy, the US and UK during the COVID-19 pandemic. *Journal of Trauma & Dissociation, 21*(5), 513–519. https://doi.org/10.1080/15299732.2020.1787296

Matthewman, S., & Huppatz, K. (2020). A sociology of COVID-19. *Journal of Sociology, 56*(4). https://doi.org/10.1177/1440783320939416

Pickering, M. (2004). Experience as horizon: Koselleck, expectation and historical time. *Cultural Studies, 18*(2–3), 271–289. https://doi.org/10.1080/0950238042000201518

Plummer, K. (2001). *Documents of life 2: An invitation to a critical humanism.* Sage.

Salvatore, S., Valsiner J., & Veltri, G. A. (2019). The theoretical and methodological framework. Semiotic cultural psychology, symbolic universes and lines of semiotic forces. In S. Salvatore,

V. Fini, T. Mannarini, J. Valsiner, & G. Veltri (Eds.), *Symbolic universes in time of (post) crisis. Culture in policy making: The symbolic universes of social action* (pp. 25–49). Springer. https://doi.org/10.1007/978-3-030-19497-0_2

Stanley, L. (2004). The Epistolarium: On theorizing letters and correspondences. *Auto/Biography, 12*(3), 201–235. https://doi.org/10.1191/0967550704ab014oa

Stanley, L. (2015). The death of the letter? Epistolary intent, letterness and the many ends of letterwriting. *Cultural Sociology, 9*(2), 240–255. https://doi.org/10.1177/1749975515573267

Stenner, P. (2017). *Liminality and experience: A transdisciplinary approach to the psychosocial.* Palgrave Macmillan.

Tamboukou, M. (2011). Interfaces in narrative research: Letters as technologies of the self and as traces of social forces. *Qualitative Research, 11*(5), 625–641. https://doi.org/10.1177/1468794111413493

Tamboukou, M. (2020). Epistolary lives: Fragments, sensibility, assemblages in auto/biographical research. In A. Chapell & J. M. Parsons (Eds.) *The Palgrave handbook of auto/biography.* 157-164. Basingstoke: Palgrave.

Tateo, L., Marsico, G., & Valsiner, J. (2022). The pandemic atmos-fear. *International Perspectives in Psychology: Research, Practice, Consultation, 11*(2), 125–133. doi: 10.1027/2157-3891/a000041

Thorndahl, K. L., & Frandsen, L. N. (2020). Logged in while locked down: Exploring the influence of digital technologies in the time of Corona. *Qualitative Inquiry*, Sep; 27(7): 870–877. https://doi.org/10.1177/1077800420960176

Wagner-Pacifici, R. (2010). Theorizing the restlessness of events. *American Journal of Sociology, 115*(5), 1351–1386. https://doi.org/10.1086/651299

FOUR

LMK, Blue-Heart Emoji & Smiling Face: Using SMS Pedagogy Amid the COVID-19 Pandemic

Ezequiel Korin

It turns out you can keep Spring from coming

I HAVE ALWAYS ATTEMPTED TO BUILD strong relationships with students. Outside of class, it is common to see them around my office or lounging on my couch, talking about school or projects, asking for advice about courses or internships, or grabbing a cup of coffee and chatting. On my teaching days, I arrive early to the classroom and informally talk with some as others trickle in. Once the clock marks the beginning of class, I retreat to the safety of the proscenium, a space solely reserved for me. It feels like going on stage, effortlessly reconstituting the distance with my students. That is when and where I begin performing the role of instructor in its more formal conception.

As the 2020 spring semester begins to unravel and my pre-class informal conversations become more common, the rumbling down the grapevine is unequivocal: fully remote instruction looms over us. Like many of my colleagues, I begin to consider how to support students once we must abandon our classrooms. Some will create open discussions on their learning management system (LMS). Others will record short videos for institutional social media. Yet others will opt for establishing one-to-one channels of communication with students. This latter category, with its challenges and rewards, tenuous shifting limits, and renegotiation of instructor–learner power relations, is where I will situate myself.

Since early March, I have been reading about teachers in Venezuela who have resorted to short messaging apps to solve spotty or nonexistent internet service amid school closures during the pandemic, a seemingly innovative remedy to this crisis. However, messaging apps have been amply used for pedagogical purposes before: from the creation of low-cost and maintenance m-Learning solutions (Tretiakov & Kinshuk, 2005) to fostering classroom interaction (Gan & Balakrishnan, 2017; Meurant, 2007; Shen et al., 2008) and participation (Scornavacca et al., 2009), to expanding the pedagogical experience beyond the classroom (Kennedy & Levy, 2008), providing needed additional tutoring (Hrastinski et al., 2014), and even as on-demand support for teachers-in-training (Ajuwon et al., 2018).

Certainly, my situation is not as dire as that of my Venezuelan colleagues, nor am I focused on pedagogical innovation. Like Horstmanshof (2004), my goal is to stay in touch and provide my students with personal support, and—rather than stale emails that will languish unread—short, instant, personal messages seem to be better. Before lockdowns were a remote possibility, I scribbled my cellphone number on the whiteboard for students. "Just in case . . . ," I told them. In the past, I hadn't minded giving out my personal number to small classes or specific students, although my syllabi and emails included only my office number. This allowed me to set boundaries between work and my private life, and, besides, so few students had ever texted me—let alone called—that the stakes did not seem daunting.

In March, we shift to remote instruction, and I am left without those informal conversations before class or the impromptu meetings in my office that fill the interstices of my performance as an instructor. I am also left without that safe space of the proscenium. Instead, now I retreat to a corner of my house, where a small desk in my bedroom serves as my office and classroom, my meeting place, and, somehow, my safe space.

The first weeks of online classes are uneventful. I have opted for an asynchronous teaching model for my media-production course, convinced that short videos instead of live lectures will represent a better pedagogical experience, as they allow for more polished demonstrations. I write the script, source the graphic material, record my voiceover, edit, encode, and upload. Each half-hour lecture requires 8 to 10 hours of work, but the resulting product seems worth it. With not much more to do than doomscroll through ever-worsening news or pace through our apartment, I focus on grading assignments and creating what I can only hope are engaging video lectures. After each one, students do practical exercises, but only a handful require some form of additional support. The comments section of each assignment becomes increasingly populated with my detailed feedback—feedback yearning for a reply that never arrives, a castaway's message incessantly bobbing in the ether of our LMS.

In trying to make the course more manageable for my students, I have unwittingly fallen into a trap of my own making. Bygone is the building of personal bridges, the immediate feedback of everyday interactions. At the end of each feedback entry or email, I remind students they can text me—a desperate call for attention, an imploration for some form of human contact. It is a denunciation of everything I fear has been lost amid the forceful abandonment of our lecture halls and offices for a retreat to its aseptic online and remote correlates.

Three weeks into lockdown, 11:42 p.m. "This good?" reads Lucy's message, accompanied by a link. A few clicks and a short audio clip later, I respond. "Yes! That's exactly it! Watch out for the fade-ins, tho. If you have any questions, LMK" and hit send, not before adding a blue-heart emoji and a smiling face to underline my encouragement. Three dancing dots linger for several minutes on my screen, giving way to a somewhat underwhelming "thx."

Under ordinary circumstances, in the classroom, I would move from workstation to workstation. But in the late-night solitude of my home, no students require my assistance. I tug downward on my phone screen, hoping a quick refresh will reveal other messages. The mail app on my phone only reveals a couple of messages from lists I should have unsubscribed from months ago. I return to the Messages app, which remains impervious to my need.

I fight to stay awake, routinely unlocking and refreshing my email and messages, but it is late, and Morpheus's embrace beckons more than I care to admit.

I rise before dawn, picking up my phone and heading out of the room. A small number 12 inside a red bubble hovers over the Messages icon in an urgent call to action. I grab a cup of coffee and dive into the messages, all from students. There hasn't been any uniquely challenging assignment or impending deadline to warrant such a barrage. I wonder if we have reached a point in remote instruction when, much like me, my students need to regain some of the personal connections we used to have. But I find myself gleaning past their motives and am instead enthralled by the machinic pleasures produced by the phone (Thompson & Cupples, 2008).

I answer a couple of texts from Lucy, who asks more questions about the audio sent after I had surrendered to sleep. Carly is somewhat lost with the assignment, so I send her a link as inspiration and explain other possibilities. I invite John to rethink his pitch, done at the very last minute but still worthy of comment and feedback. I thank Thomas for the update on his roommate's negative COVID-19 test, hoping he'll be more engaged in the course than during the past few days. Soon, a full hour is gone and a score of messages remains to be read and answered.

Over the next few days, I respond to text messages from students who—slowly but consistently—trickle in.

Marc usually texts early, a combination of his dawn football practice and the time difference in Texas, where he has been since the lockdown began. Jenny usually texts late: she likes to work when it is quiet. Lucy does, too, after her shift as a server at a chain restaurant that somehow remains open. Tyler texts once or twice before going to work to tell me how he's progressing on some assignment or to make sure I received his previous work. Mei is back in Japan and Maja in Sweden, so their texts arrive at unruly hours. Others text mid-morning, others mid-afternoon, and others do so after dinner when they are winding down. However, the most talkative ones seem to appear at the hazy liminal moments around midnight.

Before, my home was my refuge. Now my students' messages occupy every moment and space: some show up during dinner or before my first cup of coffee, while others appear in my bedroom or while I shower, when I sit down at my computer, or as I scroll through the Netflix catalog for the eighth time in a single night, invariably unable to find something I have yet to watch. I no longer stand in the proscenium of the classroom relishing the seeming protection of the one-to-many instructional relationship. Far from "widespread feelings of emptiness, of disconnection, of the unreality of self" (Turkle, 2005, p. 280), my connection to the students in this new, mediated, instructional space seems strangely more intimate, engaged, exposed, and vulnerable. Caught in the three feet between the pop-up greenscreen towering behind me and my computer screen, I have nowhere to hide, and my only recourse is to turn off my camera, prompting the appearance of a deceiving photograph of a younger me.

When I am not trapped within those three feet, I am on the other side of a textual exchange, held at each student's arm's length, forced to negotiate and relinquish parts of my former power. In a way, I am but a tourist deep inside my students' domain. At times I find myself searching online repositories for the meaning of an abbreviation or an acronym or asking my pre-teen daughter for help interpreting the multiplicity of *textisms* (Plester et al., 2009; Rosen et al., 2010) in which the conversations unfold. Other times I find myself searching for the perfect GIF. But the polysemic nature of the looping snippets, their "capacity to augment and shape our affective performances" (Miltner & Highfield, 2017, p. 4), also seems daunting, and the potential for misunderstandings forces me to spend an eternity navigating my phone's catalog. Only the GIF's transient and insignificant embodiment of my present actions (Tolins & Samermit, 2016) assuages my concerns as my thumbs execute my election. Linguistic caveats aside, my text speak (Drouin & Davis, 2009), its GIFs, and its emojis, continue to grow and take up a good portion of my time.

Days turn into nights and then back into days and back into nights with the unassuming insolence of a de facto arrangement I didn't entirely think out before its deployment.

Mike texts for guidance on an exercise. Jessica sends a snap of her health center slip to be granted an extension. Nancy establishes a back-and-forth about her failing mental health. Unbeknownst to her, she is the harbinger of the rest of the semester for an ever-growing number of my students.

Each time I set my phone down, its nervous buzzing heralds a new message. I could let it rest and wait until the following day, but I fear doing so will cause Lucy or Joanie to miss today's deadline, leave Charlotte or Robert with unanswered questions, or push Nancy or Thomas to spiral unaccompanied into cybernetic oblivion. I am compelled to provide "relational care and hope for the other" (Arnett, 2020, p. 8) amid this complex conjuncture, even if it means lengthening my days or shortening my nights, or vice versa, or both.

The exchanges with my students increasingly reference the "pre-COVID" portion of the course, usually under a shroud of indelible nostalgia. The loss of normalcy is a common experience from which a dialogical relationship is established throughout our texting, fostering a heightened sense of being together (Fester & Cowley, 2018). This equalizing move positions me and the students on an equal plane of affectation, one grounded in the shared difficulties brought about by the sudden changes in our lives.

The immediacy of our exchanges blurs the boundaries between intimacy and professional duties, and, like those of the journalists whom Dodds (2019) studied, my shift never seems to end. Before, when mobility was a thing, the phone made us reachable everywhere (Ling & Donner, 2009), but now, locked away in our homes, their usefulness becomes re-signified in their capacity to make us reachable anytime, all the time. In short, I, too, am held hostage by a technological contraption of my choosing.

But not even the most ominous predictions of the grim future for academia, such as that presented by Alexander (2020), posit this entanglement as a feasible possibility. Maintaining and nurturing close relationships with my students lies beyond any problematization of the challenges foreshadowed in our already brittle work–life balance.

By now, as an instructor, I have developed fear of missing out (FoMO). But my apprehension doesn't stem from my absence while others enjoy themselves (Przybylski et al., 2013). Instead, it is rooted in the dreadful feeling of not being present when my students might need me. My role as an instructor is contingent on having students to teach, relate to, and support. I know it is my twisted version of a pervasive interdependent self-construal (Markus & Kitayama, 1991) that sets me up for a higher degree of FoMO (Dogan, 2019), but I cannot help myself. Amid a field of continuously occurring communicative practices and always-on technological apparatuses, I do my best to catch my students as they run toward the abyss of loneliness, à la Holden Caulfield (Salinger, 1951). But my efforts, like his, seem ultimately—and inevitably—destined to fail.

I ready my syllabus for the summer term. Without much hesitation, I replace my office number with my mobile. I am eager to embrace the intimacy of the one-on-one instructional relationships like the ones from the spring semester. For the time being, my home and not the classroom's proscenium will be the site of these relations. I am unsure this is a problem, as neither my classes nor I are what we used to be.

A sense of tranquility overcomes me. I sigh, save the modified syllabus, and hit send.

Hazy summer days, what an understatement

Summer courses tend to be more laid back, a combination of fairer weather and less pressured students, who have a lighter course load and are excited to quickly advance. This summer, I am teaching two courses: an intensive version of the spring media production course and narrative, which I have already taught twice in previous summers when remote instruction wasn't even considered.

Even amidst the pandemic and the lockdown, the students' attitudinal change is like that of prior years—something quite refreshing, all things considered. Encouraged by their enthusiasm, during the first session of the course I point out that the number on my syllabus is my mobile, and I am happy to engage with them over text messages outside class.

Although my first summer course is what I taught during spring, I have reformulated the course entirely to suit online instruction. As such, the two weekly 50-minute lectures and 3-hour labs have been transformed into two shorter, synchronous, 30-minute lectures, each followed by an hour-long practical exercise to be completed independently. I insist on my availability via text should they have questions or run into trouble.

Only one day has gone by when Paul texts me. I can't help but be overcome by a guilty feeling of joy. "Apologies I had to jump on a call toward the end of the lecture today," he writes. I appreciate Paul's consideration but feel somewhat disappointed by the transactional nature of the message. I wonder if he would have excused himself had the class been in person, or if he would have sneaked out of the room. I wonder whether being trapped within a minuscule frame on my screen made the absence so salient that he felt compelled to address it.

Other than the familiar faces of my wife and daughter or the actors on Netflix, Zoom sessions are the only opportunities to see someone unmasked. Outside, I navigate a sea of incomplete faces, eyes peering above the rims of facemasks in a game of sanitary peek-a-boo. But the completeness of my students' faces, each one inside a little rectangle neatly arranged on my computer screen, provides a heartwarming sense of familiarity.

It is later in the day, and Paul writes again. He has doubts about the exercises I assigned. Although the messages continue to revolve around issues with the course, there are signs of a more dialogical relationship: he has dropped the introduction, his use of punctuation resembles the informal messages he would share with peers, and the questions—although markedly focused on the course—have a conversational tone like the interactions in my in-person classes.

Other than Paul, the rest of the group refrains from texting during the first few days. Perhaps the course is too fast-paced, and our daily encounters leave little room for them to reach out to me as questions or inquiries are satisfactorily handled during our synchronous sessions. Having become accustomed to the constant messaging interaction during spring, I feel somewhat isolated from the students. I toggle between the gallery and the speaker view, in a palpable exercise of hypermediacy (Bolter & Grusin, 1999), pretending to fool myself into feeling that this or that student is sitting across the table from me, but quickly recognize the futility of my illusion and return to the panoptic grid of participants, in which I see all of them and, simultaneously, none.

My phone buzzes mid-afternoon. It is Tamara, who has been vacationing in Florida since the course began, enjoying the affordances of remote instruction. "I just wanted to let you know that I may not be in lecture tomorrow from 10–10:30. I'll be at the airport cause I'm flying back so I'm going to try to be on, but I will have my video cam off and just be listening! Thanks," she texts. I dismiss her concerns, as I have arranged for an asynchronous session for the next day. I close with a quick humorous reference to her first photographic assignment followed by a smiling-face emoji to dissipate any preoccupation on her part.

Ten minutes go by, and another student's message finds its way to me. "Hi professor, this is Josie from your 208 class." I always find it quite telling when students feel they need to state which course they're enrolled in, even if the group is relatively small. Perhaps they've been led to believe that, as faculty, we perceive them as some sort of unidentifiable entity. "Since you asked us to be up front with you," she continues, "I thought I'd let you know my situation this weekend in relation to schoolwork. I'm out camping in a spot that doesn't have very reliable internet connection, so I actually ended up just coming back to town for class this morning and that's why I'm able to text you now." I am taken aback by her frankness and grant her an extension on the assignment, given the compelling reasons she's provided, even if under "normal" circumstances they'd be useless. But I recognize that, by now, "normal" is nowhere to be seen.

When Monday finally arrives, I feel deeply relieved as students begin to populate the list of participants on Zoom. Everyone is there but Jessy. I stall, asking Josie for more details about her camping trip and Tamara about her return flight. Niceties and small talk fill the minutes, but it is time to get started on the first lecture of the day.

My phone buzzes. "Hello Professor—this is Jessy McDaniel in your JOUR 208 class." Once again, there's the aseptic introduction. I am seven minutes into my lecture, so I quickly excuse myself, mute the microphone and turn off my webcam to answer the text, presuming the significance of its content. Another message from Jessy arrives. "I hit install on the updates for my Zoom app and now cannot get into the meetings," she notes. I toss the phone aside and return to the session to continue my lecture. Like me, each one of my students continues to be trapped within their little rectangle. Soon afterward, Jessy logs in, and everyone's rectangle shifts slightly to accommodate hers.

I miss the more personal and intimate connection I had with my spring students, so I text a few. "Hi, so-and-so. . . . Sorry to bother you, just wanted to check up on you and see how you're doing. WDYT? That I would forget about y'all once the semester ended? Nah, y'all are 'my kids' forever . . . how have you been?" Copy and paste, change the name, send out the same message. Rinse and repeat nearly 50 times. Some reply, cheerfully, noticeably relieved by the arrival of summer, and seemingly joyful for me reaching out. Karen, Lucy, and Miranda all reply, albeit with varying excitement about rejoining my second summer course. Others remain silent, letting the minuscule "Read" label accompanied by a timestamp underneath my most recent message speak volumes (Matassi, 2020). I am left wondering if perhaps, in my insistence to re-establish contact with my former students, I have unknowingly crossed unspoken boundaries and my messages have been perceived as intrusive (Pimmer & Rambe, 2018). Once again, I am left with the certainty of uncertainty.

With the first summer course wrapping up, it is time to focus on the second course I will teach over the break, the same one I have taught over the previous two summers. It is a course on narrative, which I have transformed into an exploration of self-narratives, applying principles of autoethnography, creative nonfiction, and what has been called intimate journalism (Harrington, 1997; Manguel, 1997), all while working across media. Perhaps because of its low enrollment—much to the chagrin of my administrators—and the somewhat unique approach within our journalism program, students in the past have felt comfortable telling their own stories. Some have opened up about their sexual identities. Others have spoken about mental health issues or drug addiction, while others have dealt with their eating disorders or complicated upbringings. In the past, we created an intimate space in which the process of narrating personal stories culminated in a genuinely cathartic exercise for the students and me.

As the first day of this course nears, I wonder how the uncertainty caused by the ongoing pandemic and the subsequent lockdown might endanger the delicate pathway between introspective exploration and complete emotional instability. At times, I ask myself if the exercises might be too much, if perhaps this time I should center them around something less personal to avoid pushing too close to our precipices. Maybe I am projecting, and I am the one who dreads having to deal with the complexity of my past, seeing as my present is but flimsily held together to withstand no more than a single day at a time.

I go through the list of enrolled students once again. Half of the class is composed of what I jokingly call "repeat offenders," students who have previously taken a course with me and who, despite or because of that, have decided to enroll in another.

Some are from my spring course. There's Karen, who is still dealing with anxiety and depression, heightened by the sense of isolation that I, too, share but refrain from speaking to her about. There's Lucy, who continues to work at the restaurant and keeps texting me late at night, albeit somewhat sparingly. Finally, there's Miranda, whom I had to convince a few weeks ago not to take a semester off from school in the hope of a return to in-person classes, as we don't know exactly when—or if—that would happen.

Others are from my first summer course. Tamara and I have texted a couple of times since her return from Florida, but our messages are always related to classes. Exchanges with Josie and Jeanie have been more personal, dealing with everything from the difficulties of online learning to bouncing off ideas for in-class projects, reminiscing about recent road trips, or just chatting about how each one of them is doing.

I notice marked differences between the exchanges with my spring students and those from my first summer course. I wonder if having known the former in an in-person setting before switching to online instruction helped establish a collective sense of catastrophe among us, like survivors of a shipwreck strewn across the sea in myriad lifeboats, a shared experience of longing for something taken away from the relationships we were beginning to solidify mid-semester. For the students from my first summer course, our connection was remote from its inception: we've never shared a physical space or heard each other's voices without a computer as an intermediary. They are all my students, but the relationships are quite different. I wonder if they feel the same way and if, for them, meeting an instructor solely via an online platform is any different from meeting them in person.

But my ruminations are utterly useless at this point. There's still another half of my class I will be meeting for the first time.

Before I realize it, the course begins. Besides the perfunctory presentations and some basic ground rules, the first session is the hardest one, as it requires building the necessary space for students to feel at ease telling their stories. Like Harrington (2003), I believe "one writes in order to feel [. . .] and in order to make others feel." But when one's lived experience lies at the center of the story, the distance between the narrator and the subject, between feelings and events, is obliterated. It provides my journalism students with the guilty pleasure of transgressing the maxim of objectivity, seen as the discipline's cornerstone (Coward, 2013). It forces students to muddle through the quagmire of personal emotions and recollections, pushing them to engage in an introspective exploration and, ultimately, feel good about telling their own stories and living in their own skin.

Based on my experience from the two previous summers, I take solace in the course's transformative possibilities for students. But the isolation caused by the ongoing lockdown, the uncertainty that seems to engulf everything, and the challenges inherent to the course itself add to an already tricky endeavor.

From the onset, I let students know they can reach out via text, almost insisting on it as my preferred method of communication. Between those from the previous spring, those from my first summer course, and the students I have never met, I expect to have different levels of interaction outside our synchronous meetings. However, it doesn't take long for my expectations to be upended.

While the text exchanges with the students in my spring course remain personable, I notice a change in those from my first summer course. Josie begins texting more frequently. She often needs to explain why a particular assignment or topic seems difficult to her and how it connects to her own experiences. Jeanie, however, shares her quotidian difficulties. Between working full time, trying to make things work with her boyfriend, and taking care of her cats, every day is a potential disaster.

Of the new ones, Sam, the only graduate student in the class, is the first to write. His messages meander from simple questions about course content to sharing personal details. A prolific and consummate writer, Sam seems to have the same need for interaction as I do. My replies to his texts, initially single-liners and to the point, grow in length and depth. By the end of the first week of class, Sam and I have established a rich conversational dynamic, albeit solely through text messages.

Brantley takes a bit more time to begin writing, but his messages become more frequent as the course goes on. Then, when we hit the midpoint, silence. He's missed a couple of sessions and hasn't communicated with me via text or email, so I reach out. "Good morning, Brantley. . . . I'm extremely concerned as you have missed some of our Zoom sessions. . . . Is everything ok?" I inquire but receive no immediate answer. It is Friday, and I didn't want to leave this unresolved over the weekend. However, there is nothing left for me to do but wait, thanks to the dynamics of text message interactions.

I wake up the next day and follow the same routine I have established since the beginning of online instruction, even if it is Saturday: I grab my phone, quietly stumble out of our room to the kitchen, pour myself a cup of coffee, and comb through text messages, emails, and—eventually—social media. With smaller enrollments in my courses and fewer students texting me during the summer, I finally get a chance to drink my coffee while it is still hot.

Other than my "repeat offenders," a few of my new students have also taken to texting. But communication with students via text messages has become somewhat routinary, making us all available at a moment's notice. Gone are the days when the buzzing of an incoming text felt like spotting a lifeboat out at sea, its sole castaway calling out for help. Instead, it has become an always-already open window through which I can perform my role as an instructor and my students theirs, even if both have—ultimately and invariably—been transformed.

Brantley's response has been waiting for me since before I woke up. "My sincerest apologies for not being present in class," he begins. "Truth be told, after I was physically sick last week, it kind of propelled me back into my own place of mental issues. I was really anxious being on the screen, even though I do feel confident in ur class talking and participating, and I enjoy it very much, I just couldn't get out of my head." I am unsure what to answer. There's too much to unpack there and still too little caffeine in me, so I close it and move on to the following message.

There are a couple of messages from other current students asking specific questions about assignments or requesting support with the software we're using. I chug through the cup of coffee and the remainder of the messages. Then I circle back to Brantley's.

I carefully craft my response, rewriting it several times before hitting send. I settle on a version that begins by drawing away from his guilt for missing class, then offers to meet with him and do one-on-one teaching, and finally reassures him of how much he brings to the learning community we're building. I comb through it once more, substituting a few words that seemed distanced and others that sounded like an empty institutional marketing brochure. Confident in my text, I hit send, hoping Brantley will respond, maybe not immediately, but perhaps before our next class session. Although he doesn't reply over the weekend, he's in our Monday morning session. I'm convinced he has taken my message to heart, even if he hasn't said so.

It seems that even those unanswered messages reach students. Unlike emails that languish unread for days at a time or are lost in the technological ether, using text messages to communicate with them elicits a response, either in the form of a reply or in an observable attitudinal change. Perhaps the efficacy lies in this medium's inherent urgency, in its on-the-nose imposition onto a student's phone screen, or in its utter significance shrouded in informality and brevity. Whatever the reason, messages operate differently than emails when interacting with students.

As we begin to wrap up the course, some students stumble, prompting more text conversations. I adjust my approach: deadlines become more flexible, grading more forgiving, and interactions more paternal. It is a race toward the end of the course and the beginning of the fall semester, where challenges abound and my need to be empathetic seems to overshadow any other mandate. The occasional text message from a student asking a specific course-related question breaks the illusion of me being on the other side of an emotional-support hotline. Soon enough, the semester ends.

The end of the beginning

The fall semester is starting, and several classes are still being taught entirely online or under a hybrid modality. As I am convinced I would not be able to provide a good learning experience by trying to divide my attention between "zoomies" and "roomies," as a colleague has respectively dubbed online and in-person students, I insist on entirely online. I know the choice implies I will remain trapped in the three feet between my chameleonic backdrop and my computer monitor. Even after months of teaching online, it still feels awkward to remain static while lecturing and unable to read students' body language or engage with my groups as I usually would.

Nearly four months have passed since I last heard from some of my spring students. I wonder whether I should reach out to those who haven't answered my last message. If I were right in thinking my messages were perhaps being construed as intrusive (Pimmer & Rambe, 2018), I would only make matters worse. Still, if a student felt isolated and ignored and had not responded to my previous message for any other number of reasons, I would miss the opportunity to provide much-needed help. I am torn between the choices but ultimately decide to gamble and reach out to all 50 students.

Pretty soon, my phone is buzzing with a parade of incoming text messages. Within a day, I receive replies to nearly all my messages. The eagerness of the first days of the semester is quite evident: along with an upbeat tone, most texts include best wishes for the semester and notes of gratitude for having reached out. For a moment, the exchanges seem to transform the directionless lifeboats bobbing in the tempest of our past spring semester into boats merrily sailing along in calm waters.

I have signed up for every course on online teaching offered by my institution, perhaps to improve as an online instructor, perhaps to validate that I am doing all I can to provide my students with the best possible educational experience, even from afar. In one of these courses, when discussing how to keep students engaged, I mention using text messages. I use my experience as an example, providing practice-based evidence. Most other participants are split between bewilderment and utter dismissal. "Do you actually give them your phone number?" one inquires, with a dreadful undertone. "I see no reason why not," I reply. "You should use a proxy number," a colleague tells me. "Yes, a virtual number," another one interjects. I explain that I am trying to build trust with my students and that using a virtual number would, in essence, be contradictory. Soon, even the facilitator jumps in, citing many reasons why a virtual number would be preferable. Mine is certainly an outlying opinion, and a generalized consensus against what has been working for me quickly coalesces. I cave to the pressure and agree to use a virtual number in one of my fall courses.

I am teaching two courses: an undergraduate class on media representation and a graduate course on multimedia storytelling. Although the undergraduate course is significantly larger, I decide to share my mobile number, reserving the virtual one for my graduate course. In part, my decision is based on having some "repeat offenders" among my undergraduate students, who already have my mobile number and for whom I fear a sudden change would unveil the ruse. And so, armed with the uncertainty inherent to every beginning of the semester and the recommendations from my colleagues, I ready myself for what is to come.

By now, getting the classes ready for delivery is routine, a combination of the experience gained over the past few years as a full-time instructor and the procedural homogeneity between courses derived from the switch to online instruction. Within a matter of minutes, I set up the synchronous online meetings, export the syllabus, find an appropriate image to use as a background, and populate and publish the course on our LMS.

Students in my graduate course greatly embrace being online, as many of them are nontraditional students with close relatives in high-risk categories. As the first session progresses, I insist they contact me via text messages—using my virtual number—if they need a prompt answer. However, only the youngest ones in the group seem attracted by the prospect, while the older ones look on with a sense of bewilderment. "Few times have I sensed such a disconnect so early in a course," I think as I try to address the questions that emerge. "Will we still be able to email you, professor?" asks one of the most mature students. The question ratifies my fears, and I am left to assuage them that texting me is merely another channel of communication. It's an option within the myriad possible paths to establishing some connection between them and me.

The situation in my undergraduate course is noticeably different, with students excitedly embracing the shift in power dynamics caused by opening SMS as a valid form of student-to-instructor communication. Soon after the end of our first session, the first text messages arrive, all from former students enrolled in the course. Pedro, a "repeat offender" from my first summer course, informs me he will not be able to make our next session. Karen, who has been in two of the three courses I have taught since the spring, updates me on her mental health, while Tamara, whom I haven't taught since the spring semester, is the only one greeting me for the new semester. The fourth—and last—text message is from Jason, a student I haven't met, wanting to establish the type of connection I had so longed for since the beginning of this entire ordeal.

The first weeks zoom by, both metaphorically and literally, and we soon find ourselves at the point in the semester when the course's novelty gives way to the somewhat repetitive routine painstakingly outlined in the syllabus.

Much to my surprise, very few in my graduate class text me. A sense of guilt overcomes me: did I inadvertently close off this possibility by using a virtual number? Perhaps I shouldn't have followed my colleagues' suggestions, I tell myself, only to realize the students are, ultimately, unaware of this fact. In my undergraduate course, the situation is starkly different. Jason, a second-generation Latinx student, finds that in the solitude of their home, the ever-present phone stands as a lifeline to me and, in turn, their inquiry into their identity as a Latinx subject. Juan, another one of my undergraduate students, begins texting me after my lecture on queer Latinidad. Having the possibility to communicate privately with me seems to provide them with an opportunity to share their lived experiences of familial trauma as a queer Latino. Lydia writes frequently, inquiring about classes in upcoming semesters. Monica and Karen often seek my support for dealing with mental health issues. Others in my undergraduate course text me about topics ranging from the transactional exchanges for clarification on a subject discussed in class to sharing personal stories and preoccupations.

The pedagogical turn

With the semester well on its way, I reflect on the differentiated use of text messages I have seen firsthand in both my courses. Undergraduate students and even younger graduate students feel at ease with the truncated, yet personalized, communication established via SMS, perhaps because it places me within a space that is comfortable for them. Older students, on the other hand, shy away from texting me, as though this mechanism adds an unnecessary degree of complexity to what should be a dialogical partnership between learners and their instructor. But the differences extend beyond the mere adoption of this means of communication: while younger students mostly utilize SMS exchanges as multidimensional spaces in which the personal and the academic intertwine, older students relegate its use to precise exchanges of class-related information. Perhaps better-established personal support networks render my efforts useless for the older students, while those just starting their independent journey into adulthood perceive having a professor at arm's length as valuable support along the way. I wish I could ask them, but I don't dare compel ones to adopt a dynamic toward which they don't seem to naturally gravitate and others to abandon one in which they feel at ease.

Perhaps more importantly, the students who could get overlooked in a larger classroom text me the most, uncovering this means's potential to enable a more impactful form of support. Despite its many flaws and somewhat questionable flattening of the instructor–learner relationship, short text messages provide an effective route for students to feel seen, looked after, and to seek help whenever the more conventional mechanisms of institutional dialogue fall short. However, the always-on character of these communications places a significant onus on the adopting faculty member, either by forcing the establishment of strict boundaries in terms of the time and hours devoted to this form of engagement or by requiring a complete renegotiation and, to a certain degree, dilution of these boundaries to be fully effective. Traversing this fine line required the largest effort in my adoption of short text messages as a valid form of interaction with my students.

Regardless, there were specific benefits for me, as an instructor, in deciding to implement messaging within my classroom. On one hand, these interactions allowed the establishment of a dialogical one-on-one relationship that is often absent from our classrooms due to the prevailing industrial model of education. On the other hand, the use of text messages—rather than telephone calls—provided me with a trail of the interactions, along with the date and time stamp on which they took place. This allowed me to contextualize the ongoing conversation within the larger relationship I established with a particular student, evidence emerging behavioral patterns, and ultimately provide focused attention to those who required it the most.

For me, there was yet another—albeit decidedly selfish—rationale for my adoption of short text messages in the classroom setting. As an instructor, it is only through the existence of learners that I come to be fully realized, and completed, in a sense. As such, their absence—whether due to a global pandemic, attendance attrition, or mere coincidence—threatens the very existence of our relationship, of my *raison d'être*. In the solitude of my home, in the emptiness of my classrooms, I was nothing more than an instructor waiting to be made, an absurd Pirandello (2016) character perhaps, dramatically "unrealized" by the absence of my students. In that incompleteness, a short text message with an acronym followed by two emojis remakes me into what I so cherish: an educator, even if from afar.

Notes

1. Student names are pseudonyms to comply with FERPA regulations.

References

Ajuwon, A., Pimmer, C., Odetola, T., Gröhbiel, U., Oluwasola, O., & Olaleye, O. (2018). Mobile Instant Messaging (MIM) to support teaching practice: Insights from a nurse tutor program in Nigeria. *Malawi Medical Journal, 30*(2), 120–126.

Alexander, B. (2020, May 11). How the coronavirus will change faculty life forever. *The Chronicle of Higher Education*. Social Science Premium Collection.

Arnett, R. (2020). Communication pedagogy: The coronavirus pandemic. *Journal of Communication Pedagogy, 3*, 5–10.

Bolter, D., & Grusin, R. (1999). *Remediation: Understanding new media*. MIT Press.

Coward, R. (2013). *Speaking personally: The rise of subjective and confessional journalism*. Macmillan Education UK.

Dodds, T. (2019). Reporting with WhatsApp: Mobile chat applications' impact on journalistic practices. *Digital Journalism, 7*(6), 725–745. https://doi.org/10.1080/21670811.2019.1592693

Dogan, V. (2019). Why do people experience the fear of missing out (FoMO)? Exposing the link between the self and the FoMO through self-construal. *Journal of Cross-Cultural Psychology, 50*(4), 524–538.

Drouin, M., & Davis, C. (2009). R u txting? Is the use of text speak hurting your literacy? *Journal of Literacy Research, 41*(1), 46–67.

Fester, M.-T., & Cowley, S. J. (2018). Breathing life into social presence: The case of texting between friends. *Pragmatics and Society, 9*(2), 274–296.

Gan, C. L., & Balakrishnan, V. (2017). Enhancing classroom interaction via IMMAP—An Interactive Mobile Messaging App. *Telematics and Informatics, 34*(1), 230–243. https://doi.org/10.1016/j.tele.2016.05.007

Harrington, W. (1997). *Intimate journalism: The art and craft of reporting everyday life*. Sage.

Harrington, W. (2003). What journalism can offer ethnography. *Qualitative Inquiry, 9*(1), 90–104.

Horstmanshof, L. (2004). Using SMS as a way of providing connection and community for first year students. In R. Atkinson, C. McBeath, D. Jonas-Dwyer, & R. Phillips (Eds.), *Beyond the comfort zone: Proceedings of the 21st ASCILITE Conference* (pp. 423–427). Perth, 5–8 December. http://www.ascilite.org.au/conferences/perth04/procs/horstmanshof.html

Hrastinski, S., Edman, A., Andersson, F., Kawnine, T., & Soames, C.-A. (2014). Informal math coaching by instant messaging: Two case studies of how university students coach K–12 students. *Interactive Learning Environments, 22*(1), 84–96.

Kennedy, C., & Levy, M. (2008). L'italiano al telefonino: Using SMS to support beginners' language learning. *ReCALL, 20*(3), 315–330. Cambridge Core. https://doi.org/10.1017/S0958344008000530

Ling, R. S., & Donner, J. (2009). Mobile communication. In *Mobile communication*. Polity Press; Social Science Premium Collection.

Manguel, A. (1997). Introduction. In A. Manguel (Ed.), *Why are you telling me this?* (pp. 15–20). Banff Centre for the Arts.

Markus, H. R., & Kitayama, S. (1991). Culture and the self: Implications for cognition, emotion, and motivation. *Psychological Review, 98*(2), 224.

Matassi, M. (2020, May). *Between waiting and expecting: Assumptions, emotions, and practices around non-reciprocity in WhatsApp conversations.* ICA Pre-conference on Digital Media in Latin America.

Meurant, R. C. (2007). Using cell phones and SMS in second language pedagogy: A review with implications for their intentional use in the L2 classroom. *Journal of Convergence Information Technology, 2*(1), 98–106.

Miltner, K. M., & Highfield, T. (2017). Never gonna GIF you up: Analyzing the cultural significance of the animated GIF. *Social Media + Society, 3*(3). https://doi.org/10.1177/205630511772522

Pimmer, C., & Rambe, P. (2018). The inherent tensions of "Instant Education": A critical review of mobile instant messaging. *International Review of Research in Open and Distributed Learning, 19*(5).

Pirandello, L. (2016). *Six characters in search of an author.* Bloomsbury Publishing.

Plester, B., Wood, C., & Joshi, P. (2009). Exploring the relationship between children's knowledge of text message abbreviations and school literacy outcomes. *British Journal of Developmental Psychology, 27*(1), 145–161. https://doi.org/10.1348/026151008X320507

Przybylski, A. K., Murayama, K., DeHaan, C. R., & Gladwell, V. (2013). Motivational, emotional, and behavioral correlates of fear of missing out. *Computers in Human Behavior, 29*(4), 1841–1848. https://doi.org/10.1016/j.chb.2013.02.014

Rosen, L. D., Chang, J., Erwin, L., Carrier, L. M., & Cheever, N. A. (2010). The relationship between "textisms" and formal and informal writing among young adults. *Communication Research, 37*(3), 420–440. https://doi.org/10.1177/0093650210362465

Salinger, J. D. (1951). *The catcher in the rye.* Little, Brown. https://books.google.com/books?id=FqSiDwAAQBAJ

Scornavacca, E., Huff, S., & Marshall, S. (2009). Mobile phones in the classroom: If you can't beat them, join them. *Communications of the ACM, 52*(4), 142–146.

Shen, R., Wang, M., & Pan, X. (2008). Increasing interactivity in blended classrooms through a cutting-edge mobile learning system. *British Journal of Educational Technology, 39*(6), 1073–1086.

Thompson, L., & Cupples, J. (2008). Seen and not heard? Text messaging and digital sociality. *Social & Cultural Geography, 9*(1), 95–108. https://doi.org/10.1080/14649360701789634

Tolins, J., & Samermit, P. (2016). GIFs as embodied enactments in text-mediated conversation. *Research on Language and Social Interaction, 49*(2), 75–91.

Tretiakov, A., & Kinshuk, K. (2005). Creating a pervasive testing environment by using SMS messaging. *IEEE International Workshop on Wireless and Mobile Technologies in Education (WMTE'05)*, 62–66. https://doi.org/10.1109/WMTE.2005.13

Turkle, S. (2005). *The second self: Computers and the human spirit.* MIT Press.

FIVE

COVID-19 Lockdown: An Arts-Based Narrative

Aravindhan Natarajan

The Last Pre-Pandemic Handshake

"ALRIGHT! LET US SELL SOME of your artwork!" Enrique[1], the sales manager, said with enthusiasm. Here was a prestigious, world-renowned orchestra, interested in selling prints of my original sketches made live during the orchestra's performance over the years (see Figures 5.1 and 5.2). The Cleveland Orchestra was in the course of its European tour and was due back to the States soon. "It would be nice to have an exhibit of your work when they return in March," I was told. The exhibit would be followed by a sale of my prints at their store. I felt deeply honored.

I vividly recall Enrique's warmth as we shook hands in concluding this deal outside his office building. It was my last handshake before the COVID-19 pandemic lockdown began. Little did we know that the whole plan would be thwarted by the coronavirus. Given the new rules about social distancing and avoiding physical contact, would I even shake hands with anyone again?

Panic in Madurai, India

"Our neighbor is now hospitalized," my father wrote to me from India. My parents' immediate neighbor was one of the first people in the country to be hospitalized for COVID-19. Following confirmation of the infection, the street was cordoned off, and all neighbors who might have come in contact with the patient were being monitored by health authorities. My parents received regular calls, and they were asked to keep a log of their daily temperature and to look for any symptoms of COVID-19. It was difficult to hear the news of this neighbor's demise after a few days of his hospitalization. He was the first in their state to die of the novel coronavirus (Sivarajah & Narayan, 2020).

The health authorities told my parents not to leave their house. They affixed a seal on the back of my mother's and father's hands and marked the

Figure 5.1. The Cleveland Orchestra, Severance Hall.

Figure 5.2. Cellist, the Cleveland Orchestra.

house with a notice stating that they had been in close proximity to the deceased COVID-19 patient. A police picket was set up at the end of their street. People wishing to buy essentials such as milk, vegetables, medicine, and groceries were monitored by the police.

My parents' neighbor's death in India brought home the seriousness of COVID-19 and shaped my own experience of the lockdown in the United States.

Stocking up

"My friend Anna says that Ohio is going to go into lockdown," my wife Rohini announces. Anna had heard this news from a friend who has contacts in the government. My wife looks pale. "What are we going to do?" In her nervousness she keeps touching her face, and I have to gently remind her about what the CDC (Centers for Disease Control and Prevention) says about preventing infections.

Shortly after hearing from Anna, we decide to go to Costco to stock up: canned beans, canned tomatoes, rice, frozen meat, berries, and pizza.

"Should we get a freezer?" I ask.

"Where are we going to put it? I don't think we can do that." Rohini shakes her head. "We have so much stuff in the garage, and the basement is still a mess."

"Let's assemble that old table in the basement and put down some of these cans and boxes."

That was our last time shopping in a store in 2020. We ended up using delivery services after that.

Staying Put at Home

I enjoy travelling and being on the move. I have written or performed some arts-informed narratives based on my travels with my sketchbooks (Natarajan, 2017, 2020). Now, for the first time in my adult life, the pandemic had ensured that I stay put in one city.

At home, in our backyard, we put a tarp over the porch (Figure 5.3) and were able to spend time seeing various plants grow (Figure 5.4). The hostas (Figure 5.5), for instance, grew quite a bit overnight. I was also able to appreciate the mundane—I sketched my couch (Figure 5.6) and slippers under it (Figure 5.7). Many a time I sketched without lifting pen off paper to render spontaneous one-line drawings of everyday objects around the house.

As I write about my experience with the lockdown, I am deeply saddened by how various frontline staff and essential workers did not have the luxury of doing what I was able to do—just stay put at home—so much so that my car battery died from non-use. One day, on the Instacart app, I had a back-and-forth with the shopper:

"These are all that is left." The shopper texts a picture of some overripe tomatoes.

"They are fine," I text back.

"Are you OK with this brand of noodles?" the shopper texts again.

I tear up, imagining her wandering around the store shopping for us. I was having someone else go out there and risk getting infected. Meat packers and various industry workers were getting infected at an alarming rate. The unfair nature of how society is set up to perpetuate inequalities struck me as I held the phone and communicated with the Instacart shopper. Whenever possible, we made it a point to donate to organizations that worked for those impacted by COVID-19.

Figure 5.3. Staying Put at Home.

Figure 5.4. Taking in Small Changes in the Garden.

Figure 5.5. Hostas in the Garden.

Figure 5.6. The Sunroom Couch.

Figure 5.7. Appreciating the Mundane.

"The groceries are here," Rohini says.

I take a recently emptied Simply Orange juice bottle and partly fill it with concentrated Clorox. The strong chemical smell overpowers the remnants of citrus in the container until all I smell is the bleach. I add some water and prepare the cleaning solution. I wear a mask and gloves and prepare to wipe down everything that was dropped off at our door.

I start with the bread packets, tortillas, milk cans, bottles of juice, and cereal boxes. I look at the bananas. *Do I wipe these down?* I end up wiping them and placing them on top of the trunk of my car sitting in the garage. I will leave them here until next morning. *What about the bag of onions? Maybe I will wipe the cardboard on top of the net bag?* I add that to the trunk of my car. I discard my gloves and toss the solution-soaked paper towels in the garbage and head up to take a shower.

Teaching Remotely

My university administration was kind enough to make arrangements for me to teach my classes online. Remote teaching was a new challenge for me. I have always enjoyed teaching face-to-face. I love the dynamic energy of a classroom and have always been skeptical of the online format. On my teaching days during the lockdown, I would close my bedroom door and clear up the clutter in front of my desk: I would pile my clothes, books, papers, CDs, USB cables, and tablets onto my bed and out of the line of sight of the camera to prepare my makeshift classroom.

With turmeric tea on my desk, I was ready to teach Social Work practice. It took some time for me to get used to the idea that I was indeed addressing nearly 30 students when I was looking into my computer's camera. Thankfully, this cohort of students was deeply engaged in what I had to say. I was teaching Macro social work practice. I was able to use the ongoing pandemic as a living example of how interventions are done at the community level. There were protests over the killing of George Floyd (Figure 5.8) and the contentious general election (Figure 5.9) that drew the class into heated discussions. I learned how to record and upload lectures and structure the blackboard site to make it easy for students to access.

"I wish this class was in-person with social distancing in place," one of my students said. "It would have been great to have these lively discussions in an actual classroom."

"I see your point," I reply. "However, it is quite a challenge to actually run small-group discussions and maintain appropriate distancing in a live classroom at this point," I say, recalling the challenges faced by some of my colleagues.

Figure 5.8. George Floyd.

Figure 5.9. United States Capitol under Attack on January 6, 2021 (Based on *Washington Post* Footage).

Beginning to Venture Out

After a period of strictly staying in the house, we began to venture out. We started making small outings to the Nature Center (Figure 5.10) close by. My daughter Nila enjoyed creek walking, so we sought out shallow brooks and spent a lot of time appreciating the feel of running water on our bare feet.

Figure 5.10. Venturing Out to Nature Center.

Nila's trumpet teacher invited us to a concert that was being held in her friend's garage (Figures 5.11, 5.12, and 5.13). It felt like such a rare treat to listen to that quartet—the nearly hour-long drive past farmhouses and fields felt totally worth our time. In many communities, playing music outdoors was encouraged to get people to connect and share a sense of hope. For a period during the lockdown, Nila played her trumpet out in the front yard. The melody of her trumpet would merge with that of a saxophone from a couple of doors down. The school was encouraging kids to go out at noon on Thursdays and play their chosen instrument. Some neighbors got into their cars to drive around and encourage fledging musicians. The children played even when it snowed!

Figure 5.11. The Garage Quartet.

Figure 5.12. Listening to a Quartet in the Garage.

Figure 5.13. Enjoying Live Music after a Long Time.

One day, while taking my car in for service, I noticed a man walking his dog. I was struck by the fact that he was not wearing a mask (Figures 5.14 and 5.15). Those were the days when most people wore a mask even outdoors. That was also when we crossed the road to avoid other pedestrians coming toward us on the sidewalk. I have come to appreciate the sparkle in people's eyes when they have their mask on! Everyone seems to have a twinkle in their eye, and I imagine them smiling.

Camping to Socialize

I really enjoy the outdoors, but I had not camped in a long time. Some friends of ours proposed camping as a way for us to meet and interact outdoors (Figure 5.16). We stayed six feet apart and gathered around a campfire and talked into the night. The conversation revolved around politics, the virus, and our efforts to socialize despite numerous challenges.

When it was time to part, we hugged our own family members as a proxy for hugging our friends. Thankfully, we were both a family of three, which made for some easy proxy hugging!

Figure 5.14. Man Walking Dog.

Figure 5.15. Man without Mask.

Figure 5.16. Camping to Socialize.

Figure 5.17. Setting Up Tent in the Garage.

I had not visited my in-laws since the lockdown began. My wife and I said that we would visit only if they agreed to our plan to stay in a tent in their garage (Figures 5.17 and 5.18). We would not be happy if we ended up compromising their health and wellness by flouting CDC guidelines on avoiding folks vulnerable to a COVID-19 infection.

Figure 5.18. Camping in the Garage.

There was a bite to the mid-October breeze that warranted rolling out some space heaters. A makeshift dining area was assembled, and we sat around the table in masks. We kept a ventilator open and a fan on to keep the air moving. I pulled my mask down to dig into some hot dosai and sambar.

"Wow, this is the longest you guys have gone without seeing us," my mother-in-law says.

"Yeah, it's been so long! It's weird not to give you a hug," Rohini says.

"How are your parents doing in India, Arvindh?"

"Well, as you know, one of the first COVID deaths in Tamil Nadu was my parents' immediate neighbor. That news did rattle all of us. Their whole community was in shock. My parents are OK now. They are strictly following the stay-at-home order and trying to stay positive."

As of this writing, I have not been to India to visit my parents, sister, close relatives, and friends in over three years.

Writing

I read *Evocative Autoethnography* (Bochner & Ellis, 2016) over and over again during the lockdown. Anytime I feel stuck with my writing, I go to that book. One day I hope to attend one of their in-person workshops at the International Congress of Qualitative Inquiry (ICQI). I also find inspiration in Natalie Goldberg's *Wild Mind—Living the Writer's Life* (1990), a book I read decades ago in India.

Having enjoyed the challenge of teaching online as a result of the pandemic, I decided to take on the role of a student in Natalie's online course (Figures 5.19 and 5.20). The idea of writing and connecting with people from all over the world was quite appealing. People from different time zones got together twice a week for about 6 weeks and shared their timed writing with each other.

Figure 5.19. Natalie Goldberg Remembers John Lewis (Zoom class).

Figure 5.20. Natalie Goldberg's Writing Class on Zoom.

Vaccines Arrive!

Finally, there was some hope. Vaccines were around the corner, and students were getting ready to graduate (Figure 5.21). In my social work practice class, we talked about how various teams of scientists and pharmaceutical companies had worked hard to get the vaccines into production. "Folks, this is an example of successful Social Planning taking place in our community," I told my students. There was a sense of optimism in the air. There was also widespread division in society about mandates.

"It's not even a mandate—employees are being told that they can either vaccinate or come in for regular testing," a student said while we were discussing the controversy over vaccines.

"Remember, in social planning, we talked about how experts come up with a plan of intervention based on current best evidence. However, it looks like a section of the population does not want to trust the opinion of experts in thc field."

Another student chimed in: "I read that people would rather ingest Ivermectin [used to de-worm horses] than take the word of scientists and trust the vaccine."

Figure 5.21. Virtual Graduation Ceremony.

I was deeply moved by the dedication of volunteers who worked at the vaccination site (Figures 5.22 and 5.23). Every person we interacted with showed how much they cared about us. They were happy to do their part to get the community vaccinated. There was a sense of excitement in the air—a mother was taking a quick picture of her child with a "Vaccinated Against COVID-19" sticker (Figures 5.24 and 5.25).

Figure 5.22. Waiting in Line to Get Vaccinated.

Figure 5.23. Volunteers at the Vaccination Site.

Figure 5.24. Mother Excited about Child Getting Vaccinated.

Figure 5.25. Vaccinated against COVID-19.

There were ushers who directed us to the right table to get our insurance verified, registered nurses who administered the shot (Figure 5.26), and volunteers who checked to make sure that people did not have an adverse reaction to the shot. There were also many people who thoroughly cleaned every surface in the waiting room (Figure 5.27).

I struck up a conversation with some ER (Emergency Room) professionals and volunteers. I told them that they were true heroes for dedicating their time and energy to the vaccination site. As a small token of my appreciation, I did some quick sketches for them (Figure 5.28).

Figure 5.26. Registered Nurse Prepares the COVID-19 Vaccine Shot.

Figure 5.27. Volunteer Disinfecting Chair.

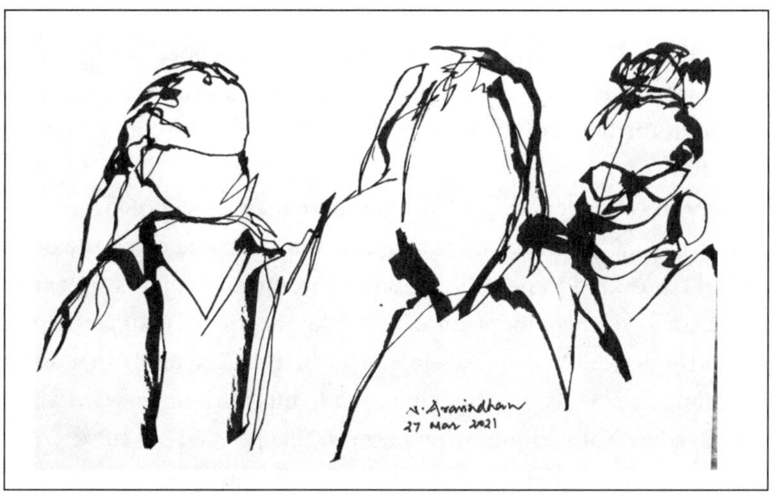

Figure 5.28. Thanks to Essential Workers, Volunteers, and Medical Personnel Working at the Vaccination Site.

Quality Time with Family

Even though we were all together at home during the lockdown, each of us had our own orbit. Rohini was working remotely, and Nila's middle school was completely online. So we all had our space set up for our work and rarely interacted with each other during the day. Rohini came up with the idea of us trying to spend some quality time with each other. She and I started taking turns having lunches with Nila.

"The Wolf Pack was great," Nila says, munching on her sandwich and reminiscing about life at school before the COVID-19 outbreak. Her school had a club that was formed to discuss various social justice issues, and Nila loved being part of that after-school activity. "I miss the school bus rides and hanging out with my friends."

"What I *don't* miss is the active shooter trainings we did at school!"

"Me too! I had to go through that A.L.I.C.E. training at my university," I reply.

"What do you miss, Appa?" Nila asks me.

"I miss walking into a classroom and overhearing snatches of student conversations. I miss spontaneous interaction with colleagues—some of whom enjoyed playing silly pranks on each other."

"Like what?"

"Well, sometimes Tom would discretely place a small rubber ball over my propped door when I left my room. When I came back and absentmindedly pushed the door, the ball would land on my head! He got me several times over the past few years!"

"Well, you professors seem to goof around more than us school kids!"

I began taking Nila to various Metroparks so that we could enjoy the outdoors and feel connected to nature. Spring was in the air (Figures 5.29 and 5.30), and we could see neighbors going on walks (Figure 5.31) or tinkering with their cars (Figure 5.32). I am back in touch with the Cleveland Orchestra. Maybe, if circumstances change, there is an Art Exhibit to look forward to.

During one of our Nature immersion outings, Nila pointed out some graffiti on the wall of a dam that said, "COVID-19 WAS HERE" (Figure 5.33). The word HERE had faded quite a bit. "Appa, wouldn't it be great if the virus could also fade away like those letters?" Nila asked me, with a dashing smile. Yes, I hope that there will be a time when we can put this pandemic behind us and go back to socializing as before. It will be nice to shake hands and give people a warm hug after everything we have been through all these years.

Figure 5.29. Spring Is Here.

Figure 5.30. There Is Hope.

Figure 5.31. Neighbor Walking Dog.

Figure 5.32. Neighbor Working on Car.

Figure 5.33. Graffiti: "COVID-19 WAS HERE".

Note

1. All names changed to protect identity.

References

Bochner, A. P., & Ellis, C. (2016). *Evocative autoethnography: Writing lives and telling stories.* Routledge.

Goldberg, N. (1990). *Wild mind—Living the writer's Life.* Bantam Books.

Natarajan, A. (2017). *Seeing the world through one-line drawings.* Presentation to the International Congress of Qualitative Inquiry (ICQI).

Natarajan, A. (2020). Art-making in public—Impacting positive transformation. In N. K. Denzin & J. Salvo (Eds.), *New directions in theorizing qualitative research—Performance as resistance.* Myers Education Press.

Sivarajah, P., & Narayan, P. (2020). Tamil Nadu's first COVID fatality: Lessons from a tragedy. *The Times of India.* https://timesofindia.indiatimes.com/india/tamil-nadus-1st-covid-fatality-lessons-from-a-tragedy/articleshow/81346887.cms

SIX

Finishing a Dissertation in Lockdown: "I Might Not Live to Become an Academic"

Carol Rogers-Shaw

THE PANDEMIC HAS CHANGED OUR lives, and it began a process filled with uncertainty, self-doubt, and loneliness as I wrote my dissertation. However, the development of my research was also self-reflective, inspiring, and creative. I finished writing my dissertation and defended it in 2020 as the country remained in lockdown. The fear was palpable as we were overwhelmed listening to frightening news reports, feeling isolated, and anticipating death. Completing my dissertation was both an added burden due to increased uncertainty, a lack of specific guidance, and the fear of rejection from academia and a blessing as it provided a demanding task to focus on, a fulfilling activity that kindled my imagination, and a community as I wrote over Zoom with a supportive writing group.

In this chapter, I will share the double-sided nature of completing a dissertation during a pandemic, the immensity of the challenges I faced, and the joys of productive and meaningful work. I will explain the split-page format I developed for my autoethnographic dissertation that fulfilled my desire to tell my story and meet the expectations I felt as a doctoral student entering academia. And I will discuss the role of disability in both my work and the pandemic.

Doctoral Decisions

Pandemic Challenges

When thinking about writing an autoethnographic dissertation, I read Carolyn Ellis's story of being called schizophrenic by Norman Denzin because she explored writing in a way that joined social science research and experiential writing. He told her that she "was caught between two camps—hard social science and interpretive/imaginative/humanistic inquiry" (Bochner & Ellis, 2016a, p. 30) and that she couldn't "have it both ways" (p. 30). As a doctoral student, I felt pulled between my desire to tell my stories and my aspiration to prove to the academy that I could conduct an in-depth scholarly study in the traditionally acceptable format of social science research. I wanted to have it both ways (Rogers-Shaw, 2020). I was apprehensive about making the wrong decision, and my anxiety was compounded by the isolation of the pandemic. Then, as I faced COVID-19 as a person with a disability, I gained the confidence to do it my way because I recognized that I might not live to become an academic. It felt even more important to tell my stories before they were lost forever. The pandemic required us to be creative in handling daily life, and with the real possibility of illness and death lurking in the shadows, I felt a freedom from the constraints of traditional scientific writing and the structured demands of fitting into the academy in a time-honored and conventional way.

Developing a new identity as a scholar and researcher that is guided by caring mentoring relationships with professors is essential to a successful transition from student to faculty member (Gardner & Doore, 2020). I had excellent relationships with my dissertation committee members, increasing my content knowledge under their tutelage and thriving with their socio-emotional support, yet at the moment of greatest trepidation, I lost that close connection. We were locked down, trying to stay healthy and care for family members, shifting from face-to-face learning to online education, and worried about the threat of death looming outside. We communicated through email and met infrequently on Zoom, but the intense focus on research was gone. Our interactions were filled with health-related hopes and reassurances, not the intricacies of using a critical disability lens in an autoethnography. My online social network became essential.

Peer Support Group

Before the pandemic, I met with classmates to work together in a congenial cafe. We sat around long tables or crammed into booths and debated the application of a theoretical framework or the difference between method and methodology. We opened our laptops or notebooks and wrote for hours, taking breaks to gossip, laugh, express frustration, and seek assistance. Peers can offer important support for doctoral students, and as the pandemic raged, we moved online.

We met regularly on Zoom. We felt less isolated and more connected to our endeavors as doctoral students. These social connections were essential to our "capacity to recognize and manage emotions, solve problems effectively, and establish positive relationships with others, competencies that clearly are essential for all students" (Elias, 2003, p. 234), and especially important for doctoral candidates during the pandemic.

When we lost our face-to-face collegial experiences, we built a Community of Inquiry (CoI). Social, cognitive, and teaching presence are elements of a CoI. It "goes beyond accessing information and focuses on the elements of an educational experience that facilitate the creation of communities of learners actively and collaboratively engaged in exploring, creating meaning, and confirming understanding" (Garrison, 2009). The theory behind a CoI posits that deep learning occurs within an online community when learners become reflective thinkers and engaged discussion participants (Garrison, 2009). We benefitted from the cognitive and teaching presence of our community as we delved into content and learned from each other. Social presence, our emotional responses to each other and open communication that was founded on trust and affection, brought us together, helped us overcome obstacles in our academic paths, and offered a respite from the tragedies surrounding us; it assisted in developing our identities as scholarly researchers (Maddrell et al., 2017).

Our situation of completing doctoral research and dissertation writing during a pandemic was unique, yet we clearly recognized that "past experiences, emotions, relationships, mind-set, and self-concept impact the quality of a doctoral student's experiences as much as ability [and affect] student's perceptions of [themselves], as well as [their] perceptions of how others perceive [them]" (Carr-Chellman & Rogers-Shaw, 2017). We had to overcome the challenges faced by all doctoral students, but we faced additional obstacles due to the pandemic. Specific direction to overcome ambiguity in the process would have typically been provided by faculty mentors, but the separation from our doctoral program resulting from COVID-19 led to our seeking a new way to advance. Our CoI provided crucial support.

Writing About Disability

When I first began to fear the very real possibility of death from COVID-19, I read about rationing healthcare and "send[ing] the disabled to the back of the line" (Ne'eman, 2020, para. 3). I saw disabled individuals fighting for treatment. I was inspired. The stark news stories of "devastating ableist violence—eugenicist triage protocols, mass death in residential institutions and the normalization of disabled death" (Linton, 2021, para. 1)—brought to the forefront the importance of disability research that increases both understanding of disabled lives and empathy for marginalized individuals.

I thought about becoming part of academia as a researcher who could write traditional scholarly articles filled with empirical studies, citations referencing leaders in the field, and theoretical concepts, yet also a researcher who could tell a moving story that evoked empathy and understanding. With the heartache of the pandemic all around, I was determined to stake my claim as an academic researcher before I succumbed to COVID-19. Therefore, like Denzin (2006), "I [wrote] my version of autoethnography" (p. 426) and designed a dissertation that joined my two, sometimes competing, goals.

The Split-Page Autoethnography Format

Storytelling

My life has been filled with a love of stories from lazy summer afternoons during childhood, stretched out on a blanket on the backyard lawn reading Nancy Drew books, to studying literature as both an undergraduate and graduate student, to teaching high school English for over 30 years. In my dissertation, I wanted to be a storyteller who wrote with emotion and vulnerability, as well as a researcher who examined the broader sociocultural context of my stories. I decided to structure my dissertation by splitting each page with evocative stories told across the top and corresponding analysis across the bottom, joining the goals and methods of both evocative and analytic autoethnography. My stories became my research, and I came to know myself; I recognized the meaning I made through the narrative process (Bochner & Ellis, 2016a, 2016b; Clark, 2010; Clark & Rossiter, 2008; Rogers-Shaw, 2020).

Autoethnography creates meaning through narrative wherein both the writing process and the resulting story offer ways to learn: "[S]tories can be used to understand content, ourselves, and the world in which we live. . . . They enable us to make sense of our experience" (Merriam & Baumgartner, 2020, p. 266). My dissertation relates my experiences with disability and examines those narratives in the context of an ableist society. Autoethnography provided the means to research disability through a study of my life experiences.

With every personal story I write, I am fearful that no one will read it, but I believe that if I take that risk, readers may recognize their own vulnerability and understand me and others with disabilities just a little bit more. I believe that an emotional response is the first step toward understanding and empathy as we make connections with each other.

The Autoethnography Continuum

In autoethnographic research, the researcher is the subject of the study, yet there are significant differences in types of autoethnography. Autoethnographers "distinguish themselves from one another by separating evocative from analytic autoethnography. Analytic autoethnographers focus on developing theoretical explanations of broader social phenomena, whereas evocative autoethnographers focus on narrative presentations that open up conversations and evoke emotional responses" (Ellingson & Ellis, 2008, p. 445). I had to decide whether I would be an evocative or analytic autoethnographer.

A nagging doubt that I experienced was whether my story was worth reading, whether it would contribute to the research literature. Running through my head were Mitch Allen's comments: "Why is your story more valid than anyone else's? What makes your story more valid is that you are a researcher. You have a set of theoretical and methodological tools and a research literature to use. That's your advantage" (Mitch Allen, personal interview, May 4, 2006, as cited in Ellis et al., 2011, p. 276). I wasn't sure that I really could use the methodological tools of a researcher to make my story valid in academia.

This self-doubt was heightened by questions about where on the continuum I belong. Storytelling is very appealing to me, as artistry and creativity are central to the process in evocative autoethnography (Bochner & Ellis, 2016a); yet, as a doctoral student, I also appreciated the emphasis on analysis and cultural connections in analytical autoethnography (Anderson, 2006). In finding my place, I devised the split-page format.

Evocative. As an individual with a disability, accessibility of my research was a concern. I did not want to write a depersonalized manuscript that would only be understood by scholars as it focused on objective facts and lacked emotion. I wanted to "sensitize readers to issues of identity politics, to experiences shrouded in silence, and to forms of representation that deepen our capacity to empathize with people who are different from us" (Ellis et al., 2011, p. 274). Autoethnographers understand that subjectivity is always part of research, as researchers decide on the topic, questions, methods, and setting, and their choices are determined by personal experience (Ellis et al., 2011). My interest in studying individuals with disabilities comes from having a disability, having a child with a disability, and teaching students with disabilities. Despite striving for objectivity, researchers are never entirely neutral; their life experiences guide them in their decisions, and autoethnography acknowledges this truth (Ellis et al., 2011; Rogers-Shaw, 2020).

Analytic. Analytic autoethnographers, like evocative autoethnographers, relay their own experiences. Their voices are personal rather than objective, yet their stories are "used, in part, to develop and refine generalized theoretical understandings of social processes" (Anderson, 2006, p. 385). Clear and specific links to theory distinguish analytic autoethnography from evocative autoethnography. Unlike evocative autoethnography, analytic ethnography does not merely illustrate an evocative insider point of view; it uses empirical data as well (Anderson, 2006).

Layered. Layered autoethnographies combine elements of both the evocative and analytic formats, providing readers with the chance to co-construct knowledge (Ellis & Bochner, 1992; Ronai, 1992, 1995). Layered accounts include multiple points of view and multiple representations of lived experience, inviting readers to contribute their own thoughts, feelings, and interpretations. The researcher's self-reflection presents a model for readers' self-examination.

Layered accounts acknowledge emotional expression, but they also ask questions about "what those emotions are, why they surfaced in the story, and what they might indicate" (Rogers-Shaw, 2020, p. 7). They are "private arguments or self-dialogues" (Ellis, 1991, p. 25). Layered accounts also enable the researcher to reflect on the writing process, asking "What emotions did I write about? Why did I choose a story that expresses those emotions? What does the appearance of these emotions in this story tell about me? What emotions arose as I wrote this story and what do they mean?" (Rogers-Shaw, 2020, p. 7). As I examined examples of evocative, analytical, and layered autoethnographical studies, I found myself moved by the storytelling and impressed by the analysis, yet the shifts between the two in layered articles was disconcerting as I bounced from story to reflection highlighted by asterisks.

The Split-Page Process

I wanted more continuity in both the narrative and the analysis, so I created a visual separation of "my story and my reflection, my content and my analysis, my auto/ethno and my ethno/graphy" (Rogers-Shaw 2020 p. 8). I provided a way to read through each section as one continuous whole modeled after Fawcett's (1986) work, *Cambodia: A Book for People Who Find Television Too Slow*.

The book contains 13 chapters, each with a creative story printed across the top two-thirds of each page. On the bottom third of the pages there is an essay on colonialism that stretches from the first chapter through the end of the book. The format gives the appearance of a book with lengthy footnotes on every page. Fawcett viewed the essay as the subtext of the stories. I found the style of the book intriguing and applied Fawcett's format to contribute to the academic discourse on disability, while reaching a larger audience through storytelling.

By using the split-page format, I accomplished my goals. I wrote creatively, emotionally, and vulnerably as I described my lived experiences as an individual with a disability, and I revealed my critical research skills as I contributed to the field of disability scholarship. My stories, written across the top of each page, told of being diagnosed with a chronic illness, living with a disability, and facing death due to health complications; on the bottom of each page, I examined my experiences in the cultural context of disability by referencing research literature; I offered readers multiple ways to experience my work. I invited readers

> to wander through my story from beginning to end, reading the top of each page, finding your own connections between your experiences and mine . . . to examine my reflections and analysis of what my story means and what it has been like to write my story by reading through the essay, point by point across the lower part of each page . . . [to] combine those endeavors and move with grace and intellectual curiosity between my story and my subtext. . . . (Rogers-Shaw, 2020, p. 10)

The choice was theirs.

Research Steps

I began the research process by asking several questions: How does having a disability affect my family, friends, and work relationships? How does my embodied learning to live with a disability represent my becoming a person with a disability in an ableist culture? How are struggle and perseverance part of learning to live with a disability? First, I wrote narratives and poetry related to my diagnosis, its effects on my marriage and motherhood, the discrimination I experienced at work, the support of friends and colleagues, and handling the fear of death. I used photographs and mementos from my life to spark memories. Next, I conducted semi-structured interviews with family members, friends, and work colleagues in face-to-face settings, on the phone, through video conferencing, and by email. Their words and thoughts added multivocality and multiperspectivity to the work, offering readers several ways to view the stories and providing examples of how they could connect to the autoethnography in their own dialogue with the text (Rogers-Shaw, 2020; Ronai, 1995).

I created a comprehensive literature review on disability topics related to the stories before, during, and after writing the narratives. Sometimes I knew ahead of time what subjects might connect, and at other times, I searched for literature based on elements of the story once it was written. The words of scholars from the field added another layer of voices and perspectives. Based on the narratives and the literature, I grouped the stories, poems, interview and email transcripts, artifacts, and academic articles in categories broadly reflecting themes that emerged (Rogers-Shaw, 2020; Rogers-Shaw, 2021).

The Writing Process

It was important for me to create a multivocal counter-narrative of disability that provided readers with "layers of experience so they may fill in the spaces and construct an interpretation of the narrative" (Ronai, 1995, p. 396). When I finished a narrative of a particular event, I shared it with those who had been a part of the experience and those who had spoken of it in their interviews or emails. I incorporated their feedback in a second draft.

I divided the stories by narrative features and emergent themes, so the length of each story section varied: the story took up one-third to two-thirds of the page, and the remaining space contained the corresponding reflection, so the analysis specifically examined that piece of the experience. While each page of Fawcett's book was not a single unit, I wanted to enhance the connections between myself as the subject of the narrative and the researcher. The reflection and analysis at the bottom therefore responds specifically to the story segment at the top.

Analyzing the Narratives

Through iterative thematic analysis, I broke the stories into single significant events, and by dividing the story, I added another unique critical step, studying both analytic themes and story content to find the best match that revealed the important implications. According to Ferri (2011), "a central defining feature of disability studies aims to dislodge the medical model of disability, replacing narrow and deficit-based understandings of disability" (p. 2271). As I reflected on my narratives, countering unjust social norms within an ableist society drove my analysis. While I worked alone during lockdown to uncover the meanings within my stories, I also found that the split-page format made the process more manageable and less daunting as I studied smaller pieces of the overall research. Like other scholars who have written layered accounts to critique hegemony, I explored my identity as an individual with a disability within my cultural context (Rogers-Shaw, 2021).

Figure 1 provides a view of a page from the beginning of the dissertation, connecting the story of becoming a diabetic while studying abroad to the corresponding analysis of word choice, longing, and story structures.

Figure 2 shows a page of the dissertation from near the end of the autoethnography that narrates part of a near-death experience and reveals analysis of death discussions, the medical model of disability, disability as loss of control, and using narrative writing to contribute to meaning making.

Researching Disability While Surviving a Pandemic

Researching disability during the COVID-19 pandemic heightened my fears, but the experiences of lockdown were also eerily familiar and highlighted the knowledge that individuals with disabilities brought to bear on their pandemic survival. For example, "people without disabilities had no or limited

Sitting in the golden summer sun sipping wine at Les Deux Magots on Place Saint-Germain des Prés in Paris and contemplating my own moveable feast in the place where Ernest Hemingway wrote, I became disabled. Staring up at the north rose window of Notre Dame Cathedral in Chartres and recognizing the fleur-de-lys of purity surrounding the Virgin Mary cradling baby Jesus, I became diseased. Ambling across the brightly painted, wisteria-covered beechwood bridge over the Giverny lily pond and imagining Claude Monet at his easel, I became deficient. I was 21, I was in love, I was soaking up the experiences of my study-abroad program, and I was beginning my life's journey as a diabetic. Although I didn't comprehend the significance of my body's changes for what they were at that time, these were the moments when my body presented its defects. I might have been a diligent student of a foreign language, but I wasn't comprehending the lessons of embodied learning. What stayed with me from my time in Paris were not only the memories of awe-inspiring works of art, ancient stone buildings and cobbled streets filled with history, and mouth-watering French chocolate from Fauchon on Place de la Madeleine, but also the descent into disability, the distressing nature of disease, the bodily deficiency that has shaped my life. Like Auguste Rodin's "Le Penseur," deep in contemplation in the museum garden on Rue de Varenne, there's always been a lot to think about when trying to manage life with a disability.

As I reread what I have written to introduce my story of disability, I see a lot of words beginning with the letter "d": "disabled," "diseased," "deficient," "descent," "diabetic," "defect," "distressing." These are words whose prefixes mean "off," "privation," "removal," "separation"; they indicate being "apart," "asunder," "away." It's quite a collection of negativity, like the barely passing D grade that while just above total failure certainly isn't a mark of excellence or even of middle-of-the-road proficiency. Yet they are word choices that reflect my gut reaction to being disabled. I recognize there are individuals for whom disability has some positive aspects; they become disabled and make positive life changes, acknowledge what is truly important to them, recognize the value of their differences, or embrace skills that come with their disabilities. This is not my experience.

When I think back on this moment in my life, I can see it as the beginning of my longing to belong with the healthy, the normal. Pehler et al. (2014) described longing in relation to loss. This type of longing is often felt by those with chronic or fatal illnesses who long to go back to the healthy lives they led before receiving their diagnoses. Longing is

> *the earnest, heartfelt desire for something, some state, or some relationship, without which one's life does not feel complete. It appears as a disconnection within a person's relationships, health, and/or purpose in life due to illness, injury, disability, or death. Although an individual or family primarily experiences longing as feelings of grief, anger, sadness, despair, hurt, abandonment, and vulnerability, hope is also expressed. (Pehler et al., 2014, p. 137)*

My experience of disability reflects these attributes. I felt the loss for what I had had in my life before the diagnosis. I saw myself as isolated despite attempting to remain forward-thinking. I asked, Why me? What does it mean? I believed I was powerless to control my situation, and I was afraid.

As I begin to write about my life with disability, I see the presence of longing. Culture presents narrative structures that writers adopt in telling their stories (Garden, 2010). For individuals writing about a disability or illness, the most prevalent form is the recovery story, with an ending that turns the longing into belonging, adversity into triumph. Yet this structure contributes to the view of disability as a deficit that needs to be corrected (Garden, 2010). Part of the ache to belong is a desire to hide the vulnerability of being different and overcome the fear of stigmatization. I recognize the value of the recovery story for some individuals with disabilities, but I don't want to perpetuate the ableism of that narrative. I don't have a "supercrip" story. I have a story of sadness and anger from being on the outside and looking in the store window at what I can't have. I still long for normalcy. I want to savor Fauchon's ganache without fear or shame or guilt.

Figure 6.1. Becoming Disabled (Rogers-Shaw, 2020, p. 15).

experiences with how the needs of one's body can move our lives out of 'the normal,' can impose demands that involve limitations, risks, isolation, and uncertainty, and can provide opportunities and new ways of doing things previously taken for granted" (Rogers-Shaw, 2022. p. 2). It was particularly frightening to hear pandemic conversations about "lives worth living" and "lives worth saving" as doctors were forced to decide who was worth a

My memory of coming to consciousness is still jumbled, more light and noise than human interaction. I had a sense of my husband being there, but the presence of the professionals taking charge and making decisions and controlling what was happening was stronger. As Tom said,

> I remember going to make sure the doors were open, running to do that. I remember worrying that if I ran to do that, what was going to happen to you, but I felt like I had to go do that so that they could get in. And I remember the dog also trying to get into the bedroom. I remember putting on the lights so they could see their way through. Once they got there, I didn't feel like things were out of danger, but I felt like there was a little bit more of, okay, we kind of got this. They seemed to figure it out right away. I told them you were a diabetic, and they seemed to be pretty clear about what they needed to do. They gave you a shot of something. They recognized that you were probably having low blood sugar. Looking back, it happened really fast, but I don't remember feeling like it was really fast at that point in time. I just sort of knew something needed to be done.

And the professionals did that something.

I remember lying in the ambulance, my clothes soaked from sweat, my chilled body shaking uncontrollably beneath rough blankets, the EMT talking to me, as I watched the view out the back window. I didn't see my life flash before my eyes. There was no panic that could compress decades into a fleeting glimpse of the past because I had been asleep when the seizure occurred. In the ambulance, I saw the tall evergreen trees in the moonlight along the winding road. It seemed somehow serene, majestic, beautiful. There was an odd disconnection between what was happening to my body and what I was seeing through the small square of glass. I concentrated on those trees, grasping for something hopeful, trying to block out the icy cold and violent shaking of my body that I couldn't control.

A 2017 Kaiser Family Foundation report on attitudes toward death revealed that 92% of Americans recognize their need and their desire to talk about death, yet only 32% have had such a conversation. Ellen Goodman, the founder of The Conversation Project, an organization designed to help people talk about death, said that we "enter into a conspiracy of silence [about death]. Parents don't want to worry their children. Children are reluctant to bring up a subject so intimate and fraught" (Goodman, 2012). I may be talking about death with my husband, but I haven't had that conversation with my daughters, certainly because I don't want to worry them. It's easier to talk about the near-death experience with my husband because I survived; it was a momentary experience with a happy ending, not a slow decline leading to inevitable sadness. What we do talk about in terms of a future death is the preparations and preventive measures to avoid the worst effects. We avoid the most painful parts.

Goodman (2012) argued, "We often comfort ourselves with the notion that doctors are 'in charge' and will make the right decisions," yet for me, a diabetic who has struggled to make my own decisions when doctors do not know the nuances of my body and my diabetes, this seems so wrong. After spending a lifetime opposing the medical model of disability that puts the power in the hands of medical professionals, I find it counterintuitive now to let the doctors decide how I will die. Yet I also recognize there are times when I don't know enough, when my husband does not know enough. I would not have survived that August night if the EMTs and emergency room staff had not taken charge. By its very nature, disability brings about a loss of control over something. As an individual with a disability, I find that there is always this back-and-forth about control. For me, the lack of control, and the fear of losing even more control, has been one of the hardest elements of disability to accept. Personal control and family control are important. Telling the story of one's life can allow a person to assert control so maybe that's what I'm doing now. We may not be able to control the events of our lives, but we can control the meaning we attach to these events in the narratives we compose (Merriam & Baumgartner, 2020; Rossiter & Clark, 2007). We can learn through narratives. I can learn by writing my story and presenting the meaning I've discovered; others can learn from reading my tale.

Figure 6.2. A Near-Death Experience (Rogers-Shaw, 2020, p. 61).

ventilator or an experimental cure. Unfortunately, according to our society's hegemonic ableist views of those with disabilities, their lives could be viewed as unworthy (Ne'eman, 2020), yet at its core, my research on disability argues that no one human body is worth more than another (Rogers-Shaw, 2022). My research on disability uses critical feminist disability theory as a framework and applies the tenets of disability studies in education.

Critical Theory and Disability Research

Critical feminist disability theory recognizes that too often individuals with disabilities are viewed through a deficit model, through the prism of their impairment. By using critical feminist disability theory, I abandon the medical model of disability that emphasizes the impairment and attempts to move the individual closer to a socially constructed norm. Instead, I explore the effects of disability on relationships and identity development from a social perspective. Garland-Thomson (2005) argued that critical feminist disability theory views disability as a cultural construction rather than a deficit to be managed, eliminated, or overcome. This theory interrogates power and privilege, spurs activism, questions the effects of socially constructed and institutionalized oppression that affects personal identity development, recognizes the importance of the body, and considers intersectionality and expanded definitions of humanity (Piepmeier et al., 2014).

Critical feminist disability theory presents an ability/disability system as another identity marker to be analyzed and critiqued, like gender or race, that examines both how individuals see themselves and how they are represented by others. My dissertation countered hegemonic views, examined individual rights in terms of disability exclusion, presented a marginalized voice, and added to the understanding of how both the disabled body and social interaction affect personal development (Garland-Thomson, 2005).

Disability Research and Education

Similarly, rather than view disability as based solely on an individual's impairment, Disability Studies in Education (DSE) argues that disability is a social phenomenon with a cultural context (Taylor, 2016). Importantly, DSE values the stories of disabled individuals and critically examines assumptions about disability by employing storytelling to privilege those voices (Baglieri et al., 2011; Danforth and Gabel, 2016; Rogers-Shaw, 2022; Valente & Danforth, 2016). These scholars recognize that individuals with disabilities are "authoritative sources on creativity, resilience, love, resistance, dealing with adversity, and living a good life" (Etmanski, 2020, p. xi) whose strengths should be recognized and valued.

It was important for me to tell disability stories that are honest, complex, and difficult to share. In my research, I aim to be sincere and express exactly what I think and how I feel, despite these thoughts and feelings being very different from others' thoughts and feelings on disability. It is important to me to

> increase understanding of what living with a disability is like and maybe increase empathy too. Living in lockdown due to the pandemic heightened my sense that empathy is needed today, and I realized that the pandemic experiences we shared might provide a foundation to build that empathy if we can see the parallels between living with a disability and living in a pandemic. (Rogers-Shaw, 2022, p.8)

I found that my disability stories shared common themes appearing in pandemic stories.

The Similarities of Disabled and Pandemic Lives

Researching disability during the pandemic enabled me to examine the experiences of disabled individuals in comparison to those struggling to survive pandemic restrictions and upheaval, offering more research and publication opportunities. Individuals have both similar and divergent pandemic experiences, depending on life circumstances. As I experienced the initial lockdown and subsequent lifestyle restrictions, I noticed that there were many similarities between the lives of individuals with disabilities and the lives of the average person living and working in isolation. I found that I managed the lockdown more effectively than many others and felt stronger and better equipped with resiliency skills because, as a person with a disability, I understood human precarity, fear, isolation, and lack of control. A life with disability and a life in lockdown both require creative solutions to manage the limitations we face. They both force us to struggle to feel like we belong when we are isolated and facing life-threatening challenges. They both can be filled with fear, grief, anger, and longing, yet they also offer hope and opportunities for leading good lives (Rogers-Shaw, 2022).

Maintaining a positive outlook amidst the stress of lockdown required resilience. Living with a disability requires a constant fight against the effects of the impairment, and the development of resilience is crucial. Thriving disabled individuals prove that "[t]he ability to adapt is a key survival skill. . . . It's not the strongest of the species that survives, nor is it the most intelligent; it is the one that is most adaptable to change" (Etmanski, 2020, p. 94); individuals with disabilities increase their resilience by facing daily challenges caused by their impairments and celebrating when they find a way to live meaningfully and overcome obstacles despite their impairments (Rogers-Shaw, 2022).

During the pandemic, people learned to adapt to changing circumstances. As a researcher who focuses on disability, the pandemic reminded me of the precarity of the lives of those with disabilities and how those lives are too often deemed unworthy. The precarious nature of disabled lives can lead to increased fear and anxiety that others will determine our fate based on where we land on the disability-to-normality continuum. The lockdown demanded that individuals find creative solutions to challenges. These can appear in momentary bursts of ingenuity or through trial and error. Life milestones that are usually celebrated face-to-face required Zoom and drive-by events. Individuals built workspaces at home where partners were also working and children were homeschooling, or they had to find unique ways to connect with friends and family online to counter loneliness. Those with disabilities frequently must devise makeshift devices to overcome obstacles (Rogers-Shaw, 2022).

The life of individuals with a disability is an interdependent one: they create support networks and loving relationships to assist them with disability challenges and fears. Non-disabled people had to find these same networks through video conferencing and communal bubbles during the pandemic. These groups are vital to overcome loss, grief, and fear. In my own life, I would have been unable to move on after a close brush with death had I not had a loving family and caring friends; I would have been overcome by my fear. Whether we are disabled or not, we face fear and loss throughout life, and facing human precarity with dignity and determination is a valuable life skill. Chronic sorrow, feelings of sadness that persist over long periods of time and are exacerbated by continual losses (Lindgren et al., 1992; Olshansky, 1962; Patrick-Ott & Ladd, 2010), ambiguous loss, where the body has changed and brings continuous coping and grieving (Boss, 2007), and non-finite loss, a dread of the future due to the impossibility of hoped-for dreams (Bruce & Schultz, 2002; Harris & Gorman, 2011) have long been a part of the lives of those with disabilities. Non-disabled people faced these challenges during the pandemic when they were unable to live their lives as they previously had. As we grieved during the pandemic, I was reminded of these connections to disability lives (Rogers-Shaw, 2022).

During the pandemic, those with disabilities relied on knowledge and skills they developed by handling their disabilities. They connected with family, friends, and work colleagues in different ways, just as they might have previously needed assistive technology to communicate. They could work productively online, as they had already become accustomed to working at a distance from others. They employed highly developed coping skills and techniques for managing depression, anxiety, and grief that have always been useful for overcoming disability disappointments and dreams crushed by the limitations of an impairment. Years of never quite belonging helped them to survive isolation. Understanding the medical and insurance complexes enabled them to navigate illness in ways that were entirely new to others and to find research to educate themselves on the virus and treatments. Their experiences with hospitalizations and the threat of dying offered strength while they kept going, despite the odds (Rogers-Shaw, 2022). Individuals with disabilities have great stores of knowledge and skills that others lack when faced with a crisis like a pandemic.

Conclusion

"To be human is to tell stories" (Clark, 2010, p. 3), and as I wrote my dissertation tales, I hoped that my readers "might find resonance in my story, connections to their own narratives" (Rogers-Shaw, 2020, p. 81). I hoped that my research revealed the need "to be resilient, determined, and forward-thinking . . . to problem-solve and self-advocate . . . to keep on going despite sometimes terribly frightening possibilities" (Rogers-Shaw, 2020, p. 81). These lessons from disabled lives are valuable no matter who we are or what difficulties we face. As I composed this chapter, studies revealed that "30 to 40 percent of all coronavirus deaths in the United States have occurred among people with diabetes" (Jacobs, 2022, para. 4), so as a diabetic, the pandemic is not over for me, despite the abandonment of mask-wearing and social distancing by non-disabled people. I ended my dissertation by acknowledging that "life narratives are retrospective, always in process, unfolding" (Merriam & Baumgartner, 2020, p. 264). I still have more to write, more to research, and I am still facing the challenges of the pandemic as the fear of getting COVID-19 and dying are as real today as they have been for the past two years. Yet I also see many possibilities ahead as I move into the future as that academic I strived to become through my pandemic dissertation writing.

References

Anderson, L. (2006). Analytic autoethnography. *Journal of Contemporary Ethnography, 35*(4), 373–395. https://doi.org/10.1177/0891241605280449

Baglieri, S., Bejoian, L. M., Broderick, A. A., Connor, D. J., & Valle, J. (2011). Inviting interdisciplinary alliances around inclusive educational reform: Introduction to the special issue on Disability Studies in Education. *Teachers College Record, 113*(10), 2115–2121. http://www.tcrecord.org/library/Issue.asp?volyear=2011&number=8&volume=113.

Bochner, A., & Ellis, C. (2016a). *Evocative autoethnography: Writing lives and telling stories.* Routledge.

Bochner, A., & Ellis, C. (2016b). The ICQI and the rise of autoethnography solidarity through community. *International Review of Qualitative Research, 9*(2), 208–217. https://doi.org/10.1525/irqr.2016.9.2.208

Boss, P. (2007). Ambiguous loss theory: Challenges for scholars and practitioners. *Family Relations, 56*(2), 105–111. https://doi.org/10.1111/j.1741-3729.2007.00444.x

Bruce, E. J., & Schultz, C. (2002). Nonfinite loss and challenges to communication between parents and professionals. *British Journal of Special Education, 29*(1), 9–13. https://doi.org/10.1111/1467- 8527.00231

Carr-Chellman, D., & Rogers-Shaw, C. (2017, June 8–11). *Do the hard work: Identity development and first year doctoral students* [Paper presentation]. Adult Education Research Conference, Norman, Oklahoma. https://newprairiepress.org/aerc/2017/papers/3/

Clark, M. C. (2010). Narrative learning: Its contours and its possibilities. *New Directions for Adult and Continuing Education, 2010* (126), 3–11. https://doi.org/10.1002/ace.367

Clark, M. C., & Rossiter, M. (2008). Narrative learning in adulthood. *New Directions for Adult and Continuing Education, 2008* (119), 61–70. https://doi.org/10.1002/ace.306

Danforth, S., & Gabel, S. L. (Eds.). (2016). *Vital questions facing disability studies in education.* Peter Lang.

Denzin, N. K. (2006). Analytic autoethnography, or déjà vu all over again. *Journal of Contemporary Ethnography, 35*(4), 419–428. https://doi.org/10.1177/0891241606286985

Elias, M. J. (2003). *Academic and social-emotional learning.* Educational Practices Series. Geneva, Switzerland: International Bureau of Education. https://files.eric.ed.gov/fulltext/ED473695.pdf

Ellingson, L., & Ellis, C. (2008). Autoethnography as constructionist project. In J. A. Holstein & J. F. Gubrium (Eds.), *Handbook of constructionist research* (pp. 445–465). Guilford. https://scholarcommons.scu.edu/gender/34/

Ellis, C. (1991). Sociological introspection and emotional experience. *Symbolic Interaction, 14*(1), 23–50. https://doi.org/10.1525/si.1991.14.1.23

Ellis, C., Adams, T. E., & Bochner, A. P. (2011). Autoethnography: An overview. *Historical Social Research/Historische Sozialforschung, 12*(1), 273–290. http://www.qualitative-research.net/index.php/fqs/article/view/1589/3095

Ellis, C., & Bochner, A. P. (1992). Telling and performing personal stories. In C. Ellis & M. Flaherty (Eds.), *Investigating subjectivity: Research on lived experience* (pp. 79–101). Sage.

Etmanski, A. (2020). *The power of disability: 10 lessons for surviving, thriving, and changing the world.* Berrett-Koehler.

Fawcett, B. (1986). *Cambodia: A book for people who find television too slow.* Talonbooks.

Ferri, B. A. (2011). Disability life writing and the politics of knowing. *Teachers College Record, 113*(10), 2267–2282. https://www.researchgate.net/publication/299016963_Disability_Life_Writing_and_the_Politics of_Knowing

Gardner, S. K., & Doore, S. A. (2020). Doctoral student socialization and professional pathways. In J.C. Weidman & L. DeAngelo (Eds.), *Socialization in higher education and the early career* (pp. 113–127). Springer. https://doi.org/10.1007/978-3-030-33350-8_7

Garland-Thomson, R. (2005). Feminist disability studies. *Signs: Journal of Women in Culture and Society, 30*(2), 1557–1587. https://doi.org/10.1086/423352

Garrison, D. R. (2009). Communities of inquiry in online learning. In C. Howard, J. V. Boettcher, L. Justice, K. D. Schenk, P. L. Rogers, G. A. Berg (Eds.), *Encyclopedia of distance learning* (pp. 352–355). IGI Global.

Harris, D. L., & Gorman, Eunice. (2011). Grief from a broader perspective: Nonfinite loss, ambiguous loss, and chronic sorrow. In D.L. Harris, (Ed.), *Counting our losses: Reflecting on change, loss, and transition in everyday life*, 1–13. https://www.google.com/books/edition/Counting_Our_Losses/2mKOAgAAQBAJ?hl=en&gbpv=1&dq=Harris+gorman+2011&pg=PA1&printsec=frontcover

Jacobs, A. (2022, April 3). Covid and diabetes, colliding in a public health train wreck. *New York Times.* https://www.nytimes.com/2022/04/03/health/diabetes-covid-deaths.html

Lindgren, C. L., Burke, M. L., Hainsworth, M. A., & Eakes, G. G. (1992). Chronic sorrow: A lifespan concept. *Scholarly Inquiry for Nursing Practice, 6*(1), 27–40. https://connect.springerpub.com/content/sgrsinp/6/1/27

Linton, M. (2021, June 8). Disability, death & the fight for justice: Disability justice in Canada amidst a time of pandemic. *Disability Visibility Project.* https://disabilityvisibilityproject.com/2021/06/08/disability-death-the-fight-for-justice/

Maddrell, J. A., Morrison, G. R., & Watson, G. S. (2017). Presence and learning in a community of inquiry. *Distance Education, 38*(2), 245–258. https://doi.org/10.1080/01587919.2017.1322062

Merriam, S. B., & Baumgartner, L. (2020). *Learning in adulthood: A comprehensive guide.* 4th ed. Jossey-Bass.

Ne'eman, A. (2020, March 23). "I will not apologize for my needs." *New York Times.* https://www.nytimes.com/2020/03/23/opinion/coronavirus-ventilators-triage-disability.html

Olshansky, S. (1962). Chronic sorrow: A response to having a mentally defective child. *Social Casework, 43(4), pp. 190-193.* https://doi.org/10.1177/104438946204300404.

Patrick-Ott, A., & Ladd, L. D. (2010). The blending of Boss's concept of ambiguous loss and Olshansky's concept of chronic sorrow: A case study of a family with a child who has significant disabilities. *Journal of Creativity in Mental Health, 5*(1), 73–86. https://doi.org/10.1080/15401381003627327

Piepmeier, A., Cantrell, A., & Maggio, A. (2014). Disability is a feminist issue: Bringing together women's and gender studies and disability studies. *Disability Studies Quarterly, 34*(2). http://doi.org/ 10.18061/dsq.v34i2.4252

Rogers-Shaw, C. (2020). *Performing disability: An autoethnography of persevering and becoming.* Doctoral dissertation, The Pennsylvania State University. The Pennsylvania State Electronic Theses and Dissertations for Graduate School. https://www.proquest.com/docview/2570179451?pq-origsite=gscholar&fromopenview=true

Rogers-Shaw, C. (2021). *Joining the evocative and the analytical: A new format for multivocal sociocultural qualitative research.* Paper presented at the American Association of Adult and Continuing Education Conference, October 27–30, 2020. https://eric.ed.gov/?q=Joining+the+evocative+and+the+analytical%3a+%09A+new+format+for+multivocal+sociocultural+qualitative+research+&id=ED611614

Rogers-Shaw, C. (2022). Disabled lives & pandemic lives: Stories of human precarity. *Occasional Paper Series, 2022*(47). https://educate.bankstreet.edu/occasional-paper-series/vol2022/iss47/2

Ronai, C. R. (1992). A night in the life of an erotic dancer/researcher: The emergent construction of a self. In C. Ellis and M. Flaherty (Eds.), *Subjectivity in social research: Windows on lived experience* (pp. 102–124). Sage Publications.

Ronai, C. R. (1995). Multiple reflections of child sex abuse: An argument for a layered account. *Journal of Contemporary Ethnography, 23*(4), 395–426. https://doi.org/10.1177/089124195023004001

Taylor, S. (2016). Before it had a name: Exploring the historical roots of disability studies in education. In S. Danforth & S. Gabel (Eds.), *Vital questions facing disability studies in education* (pp. xiii–xxi). Peter Lang.

Valente, J. M., & Danforth, S. (2016). Disability studies in education: Storying our way to inclusion. *Occasional Paper Series, 2016*(36), 1. https://educate.bankstreet.edu/cgi/viewcontent.cgi?article=1158&context=occasional-paper-series

SEVEN

Reflections on Cross-Cultural Feminist Research During COVID: Guiding Principles, Challenges Faced, and Lessons Learned

Cathy Raymond

Purpose and Objectives

THIS PAPER OFFERS REFLECTIONS ON cross-cultural feminist research conducted online during COVID, with a special focus on challenges, guiding principles, and lessons learned. This research formed the basis for my dissertation, a qualitative cross-cultural feminist research project conducted entirely online from February 2019 to February 2021 with Parvana, an Afghan woman who was living in Afghanistan until August 2021. As our project developed, and the pandemic relentlessly spread across the world, Parvana and I embraced the online research space not as an obstacle to overcome but rather as a powerful asset. Despite, or perhaps because of, worldwide disruptions caused by COVID, we acknowledged and welcomed the flexibility of the online format, which allowed us to cultivate an un-bordered feminist collaboration; to create a communal space for sharing and for focusing on mutual goals and solidarity; and to ground our research practices in self-reflection, collaboration, mutual respect, and cultural humility. As we regularly met online and collaborated from our individual locations in Afghanistan and the United States, we adopted a stance of openness and not knowing, of cultural humility and mutual respect, of flexibility and friendship, and of creativity and imagination. Through this open and flexible engagement, Parvana and I worked toward a "new collective space" online (Perry, 2018, p. 6), where we engaged in "literacies of globality" (p. 1), or the "practices of sense making in fluid and interrelational global contexts through the multiple texts of culture, language, place, and materials that we navigate from our various positions on the globe" (p. 1). In short, while our "new collective space" encouraged us to focus on our collaborative efforts, engaging in "literacies of globality" simultaneously allowed us to explore new practices of sense making through the cultures and literacies available to each of us in the constantly evolving global context (p. 2). By framing our work together with the affordances offered by narrative inquiry, postcolonial feminist theory, and the decolonization of research methods, Parvana and I were able to forge a path forward for amplifying and honoring Parvana's unique stories, rich lived experiences, and nuanced multiliteracy practices.

It is our hope that the reflections offered in this paper might provide other researchers who are interested in engaging in cross-cultural research with some basic guidelines for conducting online collaborative research in culturally sensitive and respectful ways. Despite the many challenges posed by the ongoing pandemic—challenges that have continued to disrupt our everyday lives and professional undertakings—engaging in cross-cultural research with an open mind, imagination, and trust offers researchers opportunities for developing creative, collaborative, and flexible approaches to knowledge production that can circumvent challenges posed by a pandemic, while simultaneously working toward more equitable research practices.

Maintaining an open and flexible mindset offers cross-cultural researchers the opportunity to imagine and conduct more equitable research projects online while simultaneously working toward meaningful, un-bordered alliances. Shifting our researcher identities from an "I" to a "we," for example, can create a new mindset about knowledge production that decenters the individual while honoring the collaboration. This reconceptualization of researcher identity can, in turn, disrupt hegemonic research practices and lead to a shift from an *Othering*, which often results in "epistemic violence" (Spivak, 2010, p. 35), or the marginalization of non-dominant ways of knowing, to an *Honoring* that celebrates "epistemic authority" (Alexander & Mohanty, 1997, p. xl), or the recognition and celebration that each individual is the expert of their own lived experiences. What naturally follows then is a turn from *researcher-driven practice* toward *collaborative research design*, or a shift from *telling* others' stories to *inviting* others to tell their own stories as we engage in more mindful listening and honoring practices.

In the pages that follow, I will offer a brief overview of my collaborative project with Parvana, including a discussion of our research framework, which draws upon narrative inquiry, postcolonial feminist theory, and the decolonization of research for sharing knowledge production and cultivating mutual respect and trust. Thereafter I will move on to some reflections about conducting our research online during COVID, with a special focus on challenges, guiding principles, and lessons learned.

Background to the Project: En/Countering Static Images of Afghan Women

Shortly after 9/11, a static, stereotyped image of *the Afghan woman* began appearing in western news cycles. This became a repeatedly recycled image of Afghan women *in need of saving*, preferably *by* the west and *from* the brutality of Afghanistan and Afghan men. This static image was generally not generated from interviews with actual Afghan women and regularly appeared in tandem with a pro-war discourse after 9/11 (see, e.g., Chowdury, 2016; Cloud, 2004; Fowler, 2007; MacDonald, 2016; Rasul & McDowell, 2015; Terman, 2017; and Zeiger, 2011). The result of this "gendered orientalism" (Terman, 2017, p. 489), whether intentional or not, was, in effect, the erasing or marginalization of Afghan women's diverse authentic lived experiences (see, e.g., Fowler, 2007; and Rasul & McDowell, 2015).

This static image of *the silent Afghan woman in need of saving* stands in sharp contrast to the richly diverse storied experiences that actual Afghan women have shared with me over the past twenty-some years. Since around 2004, I have participated in a variety of international education projects with Afghan faculty, researchers, students, and citizens. The Afghan women I have collaborated with during this time have had a wide range of diverse life experiences: they have pursued educational opportunities; worked and earned money to support their families; convinced their conservative fathers to allow them to attend online or in-person classes; and/or dedicated their professional and personal lives to the fight for social justice in Afghanistan. They have become mothers, students, teachers, lawyers, judges, professors, activists, and writers. They have faced a wide range of challenging situations, including discrimination, death threats, street harassment, and daily misogyny, but many have also developed strategies for opening spaces in their everyday lives for expressing their creativity, raising caring families, exploring fulfilling work opportunities, and resisting restrictive social expectations for women.

In short, the richly diverse lives of the Afghan women with whom I have worked and developed friendships over the past twenty-some years have not reflected the dangerous static image of *the Afghan woman* commonly presented in western news media since 9/11—an image that leaves little room for variation or agency. Over the years, as I met more and more Afghan women who were engaging in a wide range of creative and subtle strategies for navigating their daily lives, I worried about the damage being done by stereotyped images of Afghanistan and Afghan women circulating around the world. I wondered what could be done to challenge or counter the dangerous "single story" of Afghan women as silent and in need of saving that I had been seeing in the news (Adichie, 2009).

Several researchers have investigated the potential of counterimages for challenging and disrupting stereotypes while also increasing empathy (see, e.g., Lai et al., 2014; Segal, 2011; and Vedantam, 2013). Segal (2011), for example, has noted that an increase in social empathy, or "the ability to understand people by perceiving or experiencing their life situations" (p. 266), can lead to greater sensitivity and "insight into structural inequalities and disparities" (p. 267). As I became increasingly bothered by the dissonance between the static image of Afghan women in the news and the diversity and creativity in the everyday lives of my Afghan colleagues and friends, I reached out to my Afghan friend Parvana, whose name I changed for the project to protect her identity. From our many previous conversations and our intensive work together coordinating English courses for Afghan women online, I knew that Parvana was also interested in finding a way to challenge western stereotypes of Afghanistan and Afghan women, so I asked if she might be interested in sharing her life story with me in a collaborative study. She readily agreed to participate. Our shared desire to disrupt persistent stereotypes of Afghan women through the exploration of a more authentic account of one Afghan woman's lived experiences was the most powerful driving force behind this project.

Research Project Overview

This qualitative research project was conducted completely online, and data collection took place from February 2019 to February 2021 through WhatsApp, Gmail Google Meets, email, and Skype. Parvana was the sole participant in the study. Narrative inquiry was the chosen methodology because of its focus on the deep exploration of an individual participant's stories, the close collaboration and relationship cultivation between researcher and participant, and the notion that human beings tend to tell stories to make sense of their lives (see, e.g., Connelly & Clandinin, 1990; Creswell & Poth, 2018; Kim, 2016; Mertova & Webster, 2020; and Polkinghorne, 1995). In alignment with the postcolonial feminist and decolonial underpinnings that guided the study, the data were largely participant-generated and included book discussions, open-ended interviews, co-constructed interview conversations, photographs, artifacts, and Parvana's written stories. A poetic re-storying in Parvana's own words offered a creative alternative to traditional research report-writing for presenting findings and insights into Parvana's creative multiliteracy practices for navigating daily life as a woman in Afghanistan.

The conceptual and theoretical framework of the project was developed from affordances offered by postcolonial feminist theory and decolonizing research methods. The lens of postcolonial feminist theory moves the focus sharply away from an *Othering* and toward an *Honoring* of the richly diverse experiences and "epistemic authority" of non-western women who have historically been marginalized by western hegemonic discourse (Alexander & Mohanty, 1997, p. xl); simultaneously, the focus on decolonizing research methods magnifies the centrality of trust building, cross-cultural collaboration, self-reflection, solidarity, mutuality, and non-linear approaches to research writing, among other things. (For more on decolonizing research methods, see, e.g., Doecke et al., 2017; Falcón, 2016; Mutua & Swadener, 2004; Norsworthy, 2017; and Tuhiwai Smith, 2012).

In our project specifically, the complementary lenses of postcolonial feminism and decolonization of research offered us powerful opportunities for focusing on Parvana's agency and epistemic authority through participant-generated data, poetic re-storying, and collaborative explorations of Parvana's subtle and creative strategies for incorporating multiliteracies in acts of resistance and agency. By presenting the findings in Parvana's own words through poetic re-storying, for example, we wanted to encourage readers to suspend any "previous knowledge of Afghan women and girls . . . filtered through Western media narratives" (Mannon, 2018, p. 358) and "listen and learn rather than evaluate or rescue" (p. 345).

As Parvana and I worked together throughout this project, we explored the following research questions:

- What key moments have shaped the life of a young Afghan woman?
- What nuances, complications, and tensions do her storied experiences of everyday life as an Afghan woman living in Afghanistan reveal?
- What do her stories reveal about her multiple literacy practices for navigating daily life?

These three research questions were designed to explore the larger pivotal moments in Parvana's life, her smaller daily experiences of life as an Afghan woman living in Afghanistan, and her subtle multiple literacy practices for navigating daily life. The affordances offered by postcolonial feminist theory and the decolonization of research offered us a way to amplify and honor Parvana's stories while simultaneously focusing on shared knowledge production, cultural humility, and the cultivation of an un-bordered feminist alliance.

Opportunities Presented: Embracing Openness, Cultural Humility, Cultivation of Trust, Self-Reflection, and Flexibility

This research project began in February 2019 and ended in February 2021. Although COVID appeared in 2020 and continued to pose a significant global threat through the middle of our project and beyond, we continued to solidify our working relationship and our commitment to the project and each other by consistently applying the guiding principles of openness, cultural humility, the cultivation of trust, self-reflective practice, and flexibility. These principles became central in helping us navigate many unforeseen challenges along the way while maintaining our primary focus on Parvana's epistemic authority and her storied experiences.

The principle of openness, for example, set the tone for our stance in favor of the online format. When we began this project together in 2019, Parvana and I had already known each other for many years but had only ever met each other online. We had previously collaborated for several years on an exchange program between international English teachers and Afghan girls and women interested in learning English. I was the English program director at the time, and Parvana worked as the program coordinator on the Afghan side of the operation. We had daily email or Skype exchanges in which we worked together to facilitate individual teacher-student partnerships; we navigated technical challenges, including missing headsets, electrical outages, internet issues, and scheduling difficulties; we arranged for introductions between students and teachers and watched from the sidelines as the new pairs gradually learned about each other's cultures and strengthened their cross-cultural understanding and personal bonds with each other. During that time, Parvana and I also got to know each other a bit better, and, over time, we developed a strong connection based on our mutual commitment to education, access, and women's rights. By the time Parvana left her position as coordinator to begin her full-time university studies, and I left my full-time job to complete a doctoral degree, our friendship had taken hold. We maintained close contact, participated in peer coaching workshops, continued to meet regularly online, and supported each other. During this entire time, we never met face-to-face; in fact, we have still never met face-to-face, but our connections and commitment to our friendship have deepened and strengthened over time.

As a result, by the time I approached Parvana to ask if she might be interested in a collaborative research project many years later, there was an unspoken assumption that our work together would be conducted entirely online; we automatically turned to WhatsApp, Gmail Google Meets, email, and Skype as the main tools for the project. Then, in 2020, as COVID emerged and quickly spread globally, our commitment to the online space deepened even more. We recognized and embraced the online format as a safe space wherein there was no need to take any unnecessary health risks because our meetings were entirely independent of our geographical locations. In fact, the online space offered us an opportunity to create a "new collective space" (Perry, 2018, p. 6) where we could openly and freely share our thoughts, create trust, and strengthen our alliance.

In addition to openness, the guiding principle of cultural humility, or the process of self-reflection of "personal and cultural biases as well as awareness and sensitivity to significant cultural issues of others" (Yeager & Bauer-Wu, 2013, p. 8), became central in my work with Parvana. Because our research project was born from a desire to explore a possible counter story to the monolithic stereotype of Afghan women as silent and in need of saving, it was critical for me to adopt a stance of self-reflection and openness rooted in cultural humility as I learned about Parvana's life story through her "self-representation rather than my prior frame of references and available narratives" (Mannon, 2018, p. 351). I adopted a stance of *not knowing* as I engaged in mindful listening practices when Parvana shared stories about her life; participant-generated data guided the project, and Parvana chose what stories to share and how to share them.

After Parvana told me that she had recently read the novels *Rumi's Daughter* (Maufroy, 2005) and *The Forty Rules of Love* (Shafak, 2011), and that they had helped her through some difficult times, I told her I would be very interested in reading the books and asked if she might be interested in forming a two-person book club to talk about overarching themes and passages that held special meaning for us both; during our subsequent book chats, we moved away from the traditional format for research interviews and engaged in co-constructed interview conversations where "topics ebbed and flowed into each other, and new research ideas emerged holistically from the conversations" (Raymond, 2021, p. 75). During these bi-directional conversations, adopting a stance of not knowing allowed me to honor Parvana's epistemic authority from a more genuine space, and new and unexpected pathways were created for learning about her life, her literacy practices, and the subtle connections to important artifacts in her life, such as music, art, her earbuds, and books. Learning to embrace a space of not knowing while following Parvana's lead allowed me to hear and see her with a more open heart and mind.

A principle closely related to cultural humility is the cultivation of trust; it is only possible to truly meet someone with an open heart and mind if trust exists. There were many unexpected disruptions during this online project, including those related to the following and more: the ravages of COVID-19; an increase in violence in Afghanistan in 2020; difficulties scheduling mutually convenient meetings across time and space; power outages and other technical difficulties; and a variety of ongoing physical, personal, and family difficulties with which Parvana often struggled. These challenges often created a destabilizing research landscape that made the ongoing cultivation of trust critical. By showing up for each other and focusing on mindful listening, compassion, care, and flexibility, we were able to deepen our trust in each other and our commitment to the project while persisting in the face of adversity.

By the late fall of 2020, it became increasingly vital to incorporate the principle of flexibility into the project as a confluence of a lack of privacy, an uptick in violence, and the increasingly menacing pandemic made it virtually impossible for us to continue our regular online conversations. For a brief time between November and December, we even chose to put the project on hold entirely.

As the coronavirus spread across the world, for example, Parvana's family, like many other families worldwide, eventually moved from their diverse locations to their small family house in Kabul so that they could safely shelter together: her mother and youngest brother moved from the family home in Kandahar; Parvana and one of her sisters finished their university studies and joined the family; the oldest brother left his studies abroad and returned home; and the third sister eventually left her school dorm in Kabul and joined the family during lockdown. During that time, increasingly limited privacy made it difficult for Parvana to speak freely about her life story.

Adapting to the limited physical space and lack of personal privacy was not the only challenge at this time, however. Simultaneously, many of the family members developed typical symptoms of the virus, including fever, weakness, loss of smell, headache, and general malaise. Parvana explained to me that COVID testing was viewed by many in Afghanistan with suspicion, so the family chose not to get tested, waiting instead for their symptoms to pass while they hunkered down. Although the family was not tested for COVID at the time, they had developed most of the tell-tale symptoms of the disease, and Parvana and I both assumed they had fallen ill with COVID.

Parvana often reminded me that COVID was not widely considered to be the biggest threat in Afghanistan. In the fall of 2020, for example, there was a sharp uptick in violence in Afghanistan, and suicide bombings and rocket attacks increasingly targeted the city of Kabul and its residents. On November 2, 2020, at least 22 people were killed, and between 30 and 50 were wounded in an attack on Kabul University. A few days prior to that attack, another educational institution in Kabul had also been targeted by a suicide bomber (Al Jazeera, November 14, 2020). Over the course of one particularly frightening day, around 22 rockets were shot off across the city of Kabul, and the family huddled together at home and worried about the youngest daughter who, at that time, was still living in a school dorm across the city. Parvana messaged me throughout the day and told me how the family remained on high alert the entire day as a constant barrage of rockets filled the air with blasts and fear; indeed, during the attack, one of the rockets narrowly missed Parvana's sister's dorm. A few days later, the windows in Parvana's family home in Kandahar shattered when a truck bomb exploded nearby. As the attacks and terror increased, Parvana reported an increase in her psychological distress as she experienced flashbacks to experiencing and surviving an attack on her own university a few years earlier.

During this difficult time, Parvana became increasingly withdrawn and quiet, and I constantly worried about her and her family's welfare. I had no idea how best to help Parvana from a distance, but I knew from our many conversations that she had often turned to poetry, music, and stories in the past to help her through challenging times, so I shared uplifting messages, poems, music, and words of encouragement with her on WhatsApp to try to keep her spirits up. At this time, I also struggled with growing ethical concerns about continuing the project at all. The last thing I wanted was to add more stress to Parvana's life during such a traumatic time, and I wondered if it might be best to stop the project or at least to put things on hold.

To help myself unravel, decode, and process my own increasingly complex feelings about what was happening in Afghanistan and how, or even if, we should proceed with the project, I turned to analytical and self-reflective memos. I drew upon expert guidance to help me write about and process my thoughts about the project, Parvana's precarious situation, my ethical concerns, and possible paths forward. (For more on self-reflective memoing, see, e.g., Saldaña, 2021; Saldaña & Omashta, 2022; Stone Sunstein and Chiseri-Strater, 2012.) Engaging in frequent self-reflective and analytic memoing helped me to personally, psychologically, and academically process the stress of worrying about Parvana and her family; my ethical concerns about continuing the project; and the complexities of an ever-changing research landscape. I drew upon expert advice as I wrote memos and reflected on what had been intriguing me, surprising me, and disturbing me after our conversations and interactions (Stone Sunstein & Chiseri-Strater, 2012, p. 88). These analytic and self-reflective memos filled my hours and thoughts and guided me through a difficult juncture. In the end, self-reflective memoing became one of the most important tools available to me for understanding our research, Parvana's stories, and my own emotions and concerns about Parvana, her family, Afghanistan, and our project generally.

In December 2020, after a weeks-long stretch of not meeting, Parvana and I had a conversation on WhatsApp. She had reached out to suggest that we start meeting twice per week at 7:00 a.m. Kabul time, so we could chat, share stories, and work together to complete the project. She told me that an earlier meeting time would allow her to arrive at her workplace before her colleagues did, and we could speak more freely. I was grateful to hear from her and shared my ethical concerns with her—most critically, that her health and welfare were much more important to me than our research together and that I did not want to add to her stress. I suggested that we put the project on hold indefinitely.

Parvana listened quietly and responded with great clarity and conviction. She had not wavered in her commitment to the project; there had simply been too many obstacles to our meeting regularly. From that point through the end of the project, we met twice per week, and she shared her stories privately and freely. In the end, it was Parvana's flexibility, resilience, ingenuity, and commitment to the project that presented us with a workaround solution for continuing the project.

Embracing a spirit of flexibility made us willing to adapt to changing circumstances and walk down unexpected paths, and it simultaneously presented surprising opportunities for discovery in the process. Because the data in this project were largely participant-generated and flexible in nature, Parvana chose how she wanted to share her story and what in particular she wanted to share. Some of her storied contributions came unexpectedly, and many of them led to major revelations about her creative multiliteracy practices and how she navigated everyday life as an Afghan woman in Afghanistan.

After the previously mentioned attack on Kabul University in November 2020, for example, Parvana unexpectedly emailed me a story she had written a few years previously about experiencing and surviving a terrorist attack on her own university. Shortly thereafter, she sent me a second written story about a harrowing bus ride she had taken as a child with her mother and sister. In both stories, Parvana's richly detailed sensory descriptions and synaesthesia of the senses offered visceral and embodied images of her lived experiences and her ability to survive a near-death experience. Subsequent conversations and narrative analyses revealed how Parvana frequently turned "to literature, poetry, and writing to find peace and calm but also to memorialize her experiences, document her life, and bear witness to violence and survival strategies" (Raymond, 2021, p. 183).

Because we incorporated a high degree of flexibility into all stages of the project, Parvana chose to share these stories and others to illustrate how her agency, resilience, and creativity made it possible for her to bear witness and overcome adversity in the face of precarity. The fact that she shared her two written stories of survival with me a day or two after the violent attack on Kabul University seemed to be no coincidence. The attack on the university was heartbreaking and emotional for all of Afghanistan, and, for Parvana, it was deeply personal; I could sense her reliving and reprocessing her own previous experience of surviving a violent attack. Sharing her own written stories seemed to be one strategy for her to process and share the recent traumatic events at Kabul University, as well as her own closely related past experiences of facing precarity.

Conducting collaborative cross-cultural research requires attention to research practices that are grounded in openness, cultural humility, trust, compassion, self-reflection, and flexibility. Adhering to these guiding principles in our work together also allowed us to learn some valuable lessons about conducting cross-cultural research online during a worldwide pandemic.

One of the main lessons we learned is related to the affordances of conducting cross-cultural research online. As mentioned earlier in this paper, Parvana and I were able to forge a "new collective space" (Perry, 2018, p. 6), or a communal space where we could meet, speak freely, and exchange stories. This un-bordered space is a powerful asset for cultivating transnational collaborations while presenting an invitation and opportunity for researchers to develop and honor connections between them. It also allows researchers to engage deeply in research that might not otherwise be logistically possible. Because of COVID-related travel restrictions, visa challenges, and an increase in violence in Afghanistan in 2020, for example, Parvana and I could never have physically met in Kabul or in the United States. Working online made it possible for us to work together closely and carefully without leaving our respective countries. The lesson we learned was that physical limitations, geographical boundaries, and travel restrictions do not necessarily result in cross-cultural research restrictions. With creativity and persistence, researchers can carve out new spaces and approaches for conducting meaningful cross-cultural research by embracing affordances offered by virtual tools and the online format.

We have also learned that our project can offer guidance to other teams working across cultural and geographical boundaries. The approach to our work together incorporated decolonial research strategies that sought to honor and amplify Parvana's epistemic privilege. These strategies included incorporating non-traditional research processes, such as a focus on participant-generated data, book chats, re-storied findings in poetic form, and co-constructed interview conversations. This shift in focus from the individual researcher to more inclusive collaborative practices is an invitation to actively and fully engage everyone in research activities. A collaborative approach to cross-cultural research offers opportunities for understanding and supporting women internationally in more authentic ways, especially when we incorporate decolonizing research strategies, which disrupt hegemonic research practices and honor participants' epistemic authority.

Finally, Parvana and I have learned that following a set of guiding principles rooted in care and mutual respect has allowed us to develop our personal and professional connections to each other in ways that encourage us to look beyond the project described in this paper and into future collaborative possibilities. Since completing this project, for example, Parvana and I have continued meeting online. She and her family managed to leave Afghanistan in August 2021, and they resettled in Canada, where they are now working on adapting to a new culture as they also adjust to new schools, work, and daily life. Since they resettled in Canada, I have offered my services to tutor Parvana's mom in English and to coach Parvana through job searches and mock interviews, and, by the time this article appears in print, I will even have met my beautiful Afghan family in person for the first time.

Parvana and I also recently began working on a book-length project. The project is a work of non-fiction and explores the unique and unexpected friendship that developed between us—a friendship between a middle-aged woman from the United States and a young woman from Afghanistan—that began and developed online over space and time. Just as the online format can open pathways for meaningful, un-bordered collaborations for activists and researchers who are open to its potential, so, too, can researchers from different ages, cultures, and languages recognize and embrace commonalities in their lived experiences, which transcend differences in age, time, and space. We hope our future work together will offer expanded insights into the boundless possibilities of engaging with others with an open mind and spirit.

***

The table below provides a brief summary of the guiding principles at the heart of our work together; the lessons learned for our cross-cultural collaboration during COVID; and the challenges we faced and strategies we employed for overcoming disruptions to our work together.

Table 7.1. Guiding Principles, Lessons Learned, Challenges Faced

Guiding Principles Deepened During COVID
1. *Openness* (embracing online format as an opportunity, not a hindrance, e.g., for collaborative un-bordered alliances, imagination, flexibility)
2. *Cultural humility*, or what Mannon (2018) refers to as the "willingness to learn about another's world through her self-representation rather than my prior frame of reference and available narratives" (p. 351)
3. *Cultivation of trust* (e.g., through active listening, flexibility, compassion, cultural humility, bi-directional sharing, respectful and inclusive language)
4. *Self-reflective practices* (e.g., ongoing self-reflective and analytic memoing)
5. *Flexibility* (e.g., being aware of limitations, creating workarounds, being open to unexpected turns)

Lessons Learned
a. To embrace the online format as a "new collective space" (Perry, 2018, p. 6) for conducting collaborative cross-cultural research, even when meeting in person is not possible
b. To recognize that our own cross-cultural work can serve as a model for other teams, especially those working across cultural and geographical boundaries; those that are genuinely interested in learning about other women's lived experiences; and those dedicated to authentically understanding, supporting, and honoring women internationally
c. To understand that cultivating an open stance based on care and mutual respect can be the foundation for future collaborative projects together (e.g., in our case, a new book project, ongoing book talks, tutoring, mentoring, etc.)

Challenges Faced	Strategies for Persisting
Time difference between Kabul and the United States (9.5 hours)	Flexibility to accommodate changing schedules; setting regular, mutually convenient times to meet
Increased violence in Afghanistan (e.g., KU attack, suicide bombings, rockets, terror)	Uploading poetry, songs, sayings; sharing written stories; putting project on hold; being present and available
Space and privacy (e.g., family of seven in one small house)	Establishing time/place to meet that allows for more freedom to speak
Technical roadblocks (e.g., internet connectivity, dropped calls, audio/video difficulties)	Patience, persistence, understanding; drawing on shared history of overcoming technical roadblocks
Emotional challenges (e.g., stress, anxiety)	Cultural humility; emotional support; flexibility
Physical/health issues (e.g., COVID, sickness)	Flexibility; putting project on hold
Concerns about completing project	Trust, flexibility, openness; memoing

References

Adichie, C. (2009). *The danger of a single story* [video file]. https://www.ted.com/talks/chimamanda_ngozi_adichie_the_danger_of_a_single_story?language=en

Alexander, M. J., & Mohanty, C. T. (1997). Introduction: Genealogies, legacies, movements. In M. J. Alexander & C. T. Mohanty (Eds.), *Feminist genealogies, colonial legacies, democratic futures* (pp. xiii–xlii). Routledge.

Al Jazeera. (2020, November 14). Afghan forces capture "mastermind" of Kabul University attack. Aljazeera. https://www.aljazeera.com/news/2020/11/14/afghan-forces-capture-mastermind-of-kabul-university-attack

Chowdury, E. (2016). Development paradoxes: Feminist solidarity, alternative imaginaries, and new spaces. *Journal of International Women's Studies, 17*(1), 117–132.

Cloud, D. L. (2004). "To veil the threat of terror": Afghan women and the "clash of civilizations" in the imagery of the U.S. war on terrorism. *Quarterly Journal of Speech, 90*(3), 285–306.

Connelly, F. M., & Clandinin, D. J. (1990). Stories of experience and narrative inquiry. *American Educational Research Association, 19*(5), 2–14.

Creswell, J., & Poth, C. (2018). *Qualitative inquiry and research design: Choosing among five approaches.* Sage Publications.

Doecke, B., Anwar, D., & Illesca, B. (2017). Narrative language and literacy education: Research within a postcolonial framework. In S.-A. Mirhosseini (Ed.), *Reflections on qualitative research in language and literacy education* (pp. 29–43). Springer International Publishing.

Falcón, S. M. (2016). Transnational feminism as a paradigm for decolonizing the practice of research: Identifying feminist principles and methodology criteria for U.S.-based scholars. *Frontiers: A Journal of Women Studies, 37*(1), 174–194.

Fowler, C. (2007). Journalists in feminist clothing: Men and women reporting Afghan women during Operation Enduring Freedom, 2001. *Journal of International Women's Studies, 8*(2), 4–19.

Kim, J.-H. (2016). *Understanding narrative inquiry: The crafting and analysis of stories as research.* Sage.

Lai, C. K., Marini, M., Lehr, S. A., Cerruti, C., Shin, J.-E. L., Joy-Gaba, J. A., Ho, A. K., Teachman, B. A., Wojcik, S. P., Koleva, S. P., Frazier, R. S., Heiphetz, L., Chen, E. E., Turner, R. N., Haidt, J., Kesebir, S., Hawkins, C. B., Schaefer, H. S., Rubichi, S., Sartori, G., Dial, C. M., Sriram, N., Banaji, M. R., & Nosek, B. A. (2014). Reducing implicit racial preferences: I. A comparative investigation of 17 interventions. *Journal of Experimental Psychology: General.* Advance online publication.

MacDonald, K. (2016). Calls for educating girls in the Third World: Futurity, girls and the "Third World Woman." *Gender, Place & Culture, 23*(1), 1–17, doi: 10.1080/0966369X.2014.991699

Mannon, B. (2018). Spectators, sponsors, or world travelers? Engaging with personal narratives of others through the Afghan Women's Writing Project. *College English, 80*(4), 342–363.

Maufroy, M. (2005). *Rumi's daughter*. Rider.

Mertova, P., & Webster, L. (2020). *Using narrative inquiry as a research method: An introduction to critical event narrative analysis in research, teaching and professional practice* (2nd ed.). Routledge.

Mutua, K., & Swadener, B. B. (Eds.). (2004). *Decolonizing research in cross-cultural contexts: Critical personal narratives*. State University of New York Press.

Norsworthy, K. (2017). Mindful activism: Embracing the complexities of international border crossings. *American Psychologist, 72*(9), 1035–1043.

Perry, M. (2018). Unpacking the imaginary in literacies of globality. *Discourse: Studies in the Cultural Politics of Education, 41*(2):1-13 https://doi.org/10.1080/01596306.2018.1515064

Polkinghorne, D. E. (1995). Narrative configuration as qualitative analysis. In J. A. Hatch & R. Wisniewski (Eds.), *Life history and narrative* (pp. 5–25). Falmer Press.

Rasul, A., & McDowell, S. D. (2015). Images of oppression: An analysis of the coverage of Afghan women in *Time* and *Newsweek* after 9/11. *The Journal of International Communication, 21*(1), 21–37, doi: 10.1080/13216597.2014.987798

Raymond, C. (2021). *"I forgot how strong I have been": A narrative inquiry of one Afghan woman's storied experiences*. Doctoral dissertation, Indiana University, Bloomington. https://hdl.handle.net/2022/26628

Saldaña, J. (2021). *The coding manual for qualitative researchers* (4th ed.). Sage.

Saldaña, J., & Omashta, M. (2022). *Qualitative research: Analyzing life*. Sage.

Segal, E. A. (2011). Social empathy: A model built on empathy, contextual understanding, and social responsibility that promotes social justice. *Journal of Social Service Research, 37*(3), 266–277.

Shafak, E. (2011). *The forty rules of love: A novel of Rumi*. Penguin Books.

Spivak, G. (2010). Can the subaltern speak? In R. Morris (Ed.), *Can the subaltern speak? History of an idea*. Columbia University Press.

Stone Sunstein, B., & Chiseri-Strater, E. (2012). *FieldWorking: Reading and Writing Research* (4th ed.). Bedford/St. Martin's.

Terman, R. (2017). Islamophobia and media portrayals of Muslim women: A computational text analysis of US news coverage. *International Studies Quarterly, 61*(3), 489–502.

Tuhiwai Smith, L. (2012). *Decolonizing methodologies: Research and indigenous peoples* (2nd ed.). Zed Books.

Vedantam, S. (2013). How to fight racial bias when it's silent and subtle. NPR.org. podcast. https://www.npr.org/sections/codeswitch/2013/07/19/203306999/How-To-Fight-Racial-Bias-When-Its-Silent-And-Subtle

Yeager, K. A., & Bauer-Wu, S. (2013). Cultural humility: Essential foundation for clinical researchers. *Applied Nursing Research, 26*(4) pp. 251-256. doi:10.1016/j.apnr.2013.06.008

Zeiger, D. (2011). Afghanistan blues: Seeing beyond the burqa on YouTube. In J. Heath, & A. Zahedi (Eds.), *Land of the unconquerable: The lives of contemporary Afghan women* (pp. 86–95). University of California Press.

EIGHT

Refugee Youth Amidst Multiple Pandemics: Mobilizing Hope and Solidarity through Collective Memory Writing

Emina Bužinkić

THE COVID-19 PANDEMIC HAS REVEALED the virality of the social pandemics that have also created social distance from and against the racial, ethnic, and transnational other, including in the context of schooling. When schools shut their doors and switched to online learning in the Croatian language, in the midst of the first month of virality of the COVID-19 pandemic, refugee and other minoritized youth were left behind (GOOD Initiative, 2020). Since online schooling was offered only in Croatian, the education authorities ultimately excluded from the learning platform refugee youth who did not know and speak the language sufficiently well (Kuća ljudskih prava & GOOD Initiative, 2021). These students could only join schooling at the beginning of the new school year in September of 2020, despite public pressure applied by civil society actors and refugee youths' parents.

In response to youth being cast out of education, I have been engaged in the collaborative work of advocating for the holistic inclusion of refugee youth in the Croatian education system and society. This agitational labor took place mainly through Workgroup UnEqual, an *ad hoc* space established a few weeks into the COVID-19 pandemic and exclusive online schooling. The UnEqual operated as the working structure of the GOOD Initiative—a national, informal platform that advocates for equal access to education and the democratization of the education system in Croatia. My advocacy work through UnEqual was a continuation of almost two decades of leading or collaborating on organizing, public advocacy, and policymaking for quality educational and life opportunities for refugee youth in Croatia.

I was eager to meet these young refugees who had been excluded from schooling, but the state of emergency and lockdowns did not allow for movement and connections. However, a series of serendipitous moments connected me with Aicha, who was one of those refugee youth who did not receive a single notice about schooling switching to online learning, nor was she provided, in her interrupted education journey, any support from her school and the educational authorities. Both serendipity and curiosity led me to meeting Sondan and Reyhan and their families. I reconnected with Sam, Mira, and Omar, whom I have known since their arrival in Croatia in 2015, and I have been involved in their struggles with egregious migration and asylum politics when it comes to issues of legalization of their status and issues concerning access to and expulsions from schooling. The ethnographic study came as a continuation of my ongoing relationship and solidarity building with refugee youth and their families in the towns of Sisak and Zagreb. They breathed life into the critical ethnographic narrative inquiry *(UN)safe identities. Race and ethnicity in the times of social distancing: youth refugee perspectives.*

Built on years of community and academic activism in the critical interrogation of how migration and education regimes are harming refugee and migrant youth, my critical ethnographic study was concerned with the question of what it might mean for refugee youth in Croatia to be of a non-dominant race and ethnicity in a time where the social distancing of the COVID-19 pandemic is intersecting with the social distancing of the enhanced securitization politics that normalizes racialization and criminalization of refugees and migrants. All seven youth involved in the research were uprooted from Southwest Asia and North Africa (SWANA), with the wars in Syria being a dominant factor in expulsion from their homes. Now living in Croatia, a place where the Balkans and European Union and generate strong anti-migration, Islamophobic, and racist sentiments. The grammar of securitization has proliferated ever since the *long summer of migration* (Kasparek & Speer, 2015), popularly misrepresented as the *refugee* or *migrant crisis* (Bužinkić & Hameršak, 2018).

With the disruptive closure of the Balkan corridor only a few months after the organized transportation of refugees from the Greek–Macedonian border to Austria and Germany (Bužinkić & Hameršak, 2018), the securitization politics of the European Union has been restored to the idea that refugees and migrants—portrayed through a figure of the "Muslim extremist"—"represent . . . a security threat" (De Genova, 2017, p. 13). One of the most pronounced forms of securitization and criminalization politics is the deployment of physical removals or *pushbacks* of refugees, migrants, and people on the move across borders. The normalization of securitization-related violence and negative propaganda that "relied heavily on racializing practices and the mobilization of racist sentiments in the public sphere" (Beznec & Kurnik, 2020) has affected the mobility and safety of refugees and migrants in all aspects of their lives. Through my critical ethnographic study, I was particularly interested in exploring the semiotic meaning of border regimes, that is, the translation of securitization discourse and the effects of the enhancement of securitization politics in distance schooling (*škola na daljinu*) of racially, ethnically, linguistically, and culturally different refugee youth during the pandemic. Moreover, I explored how the experiences of refugee youth in (distance) schooling have been shaping their complex identities (racial, transnational, national, religious, and gender) and how those identities have been negotiated in socially distant schooling and everyday life.

The beginning of the ethnographic narrative inquiry intersected with the onset of the second wave of the COVID-19 pandemic in September 2020, and only a few months before a series of devastating earthquakes in central Croatia in December. Between the rainy fall of 2020 and the blossoming spring of 2021, I engaged in the labor of documenting narrative experiences of refugeeness and education in Croatia with Aicha, Sondan, Reyhan, Sam, Omar, and Mira. Toward the end of spring, I met Bella, after her story was published by comrade journalist Barbara Matejčić in the Croatian newspaper *Jutarnji list*. I have spent long hours in conversation with seven refugee youth by carefully documenting their individual personal narratives. In addition, Aicha and I went on a journey of collaborative autobiographical writing, one that invited narration of *self* and *the other* in the most profound ways. This rhythm of meeting and developing personal relationships ultimately led to the labor of collaborative and collective writing.

From bilateral conversations, this ethnographic narrative inquiry evolved to the process of collaborative autoethnographies and then to collective memory writing, powerfully revealing and releasing pain, yearnings, and struggles. Seven unique life stories, both individually and collectively shared, and the narration of *self* explored our refugee journeys, the *longue durée* of social distancing, schooling amidst the COVID-19 pandemic, and the recent earthquakes as experiences of literal and figurative perpetual displacements. These seven stories demonstrate a nuanced account of refugee youth experiences of schooling and struggles for identity, belonging, and political urges.

The narratives serve to ground a nuanced understanding of the complexities that refugee youth are living through as they negotiate their identities and existence amidst multiple societal pandemics such as anti-Muslim violence, anti-Black racism, and anti-migrant sentiments (Imagining Transnational Solidarities Research Circle, 2020).

Narrative inquiry and collaborative autoethnographies have also paved the way for the collective memory writing that will prove to be a journey of close *co-travelers* (Nagar, 2015) committed to making sense of a today interwoven with memories of the past and hopes for the future. Memories and stories became the point of envisioning different futures and critical junctures calling for rebuilding social closeness and intimacies that represent stark opposition to the regimes of social distancing caused by the COVID-19 and societal pandemics. With the occurrence of the earthquakes at the end of the first year of the novel pandemic, additional layers of exploration unfolded in the inquiry—those of safety and perpetual displacement, as well as those of hope, solidarity, and imagination of possibilities.

Narrative inquiry, collaborative autoethnography, and collective memory writing have paved the way for a deep analysis of the rigid migration and refugee regimes and anti-Muslim politics imposed on these youth, including stereotyping, surveilling, disciplining, and multiple occasions of literal and figurative displacing—all of them traits of the current European securitization migration regime. I claim that such politics is not only localized at the borders; rather, it disperses and inscribes its grammar in daily interactions and social locations such as schools.

Drawing from the inspirational and heartfelt Nagar's trilogy (2006, 2015, & 2019) and Zia's collaborative research and activism in Kashmir (2019), I pondered the following question: In what ways will our group co-create the methodology, praxis, and poetics of collective memory writing as it reveals layers of erasures and simultaneously opens the possibilities for epistemic justice in ways, forms, and meanings pertinent to us as collective memory writers? In continuing this discussion, I tend to the question of methodologies, collectivity, and solidarity-making in collective praxis, while weaving the emerging experiences with SWANA refugee youth and the experiences of other collective memory writing projects explored through the literature.

Flowing in the collective memory writing with SWANA refugee youth

> "[K]nowledge grows out of and is embodied in dialogue."
>
> —*Nagar et al., 2006, p. 154*

The instigation and inspiration for collective memory writing with refugee youth derived from three examples of transnational feminist memory work with women's collectives in different historico-political, geographical, epistemic, and temporal settings. I learn from the experiences of Frigga Haug with Frauenformen and Das Argument Kolektiv; Richa Nagar with the Sangtin Writers Collective, Sangtin Kisan Mazdoor Sangathan (SKMS), and Parakh Theatre; and Patricia Connolly-Shaffer, who engaged with the cross-border reading alliance, utilizing the method of polyvocal feminist testimonio. These projects exemplify liberating, empowering, and healing journeys for female collectives.

Breathing with the Marxist-Feminist pulse, and practiced in Berlin and Hamburg, Germany, in the 1980s, Haug (1999) discusses memory work as an extension beyond the conventions of narrative inquiry, where memory work is "not only experience, but work with the experience, which is useful as a research method" (p. 2). Haug paved new ways of thinking about and doing feminist projects globally, as the emergence of collective memory writing was a practice of emancipatory learning and research. Hamm (2020) argues that "it was meant to be a means for learning through, and aimed at coming together and social aggregation. Learning in this context is always first and foremost unlearning, based on a critical reflection of experiences, opinions, and construction of meaning, done in conjunction with others."

Relatedly, Nagar's *Playing with Fire* (2006) is nested in reflexive activism and collective analysis. Nagar (2006) asserts that it "emerged from a collectively produced methodology in which autobiographical writing and discussions of that writing became tools through which we built our analysis and critique of societal structures and processes, ranging from the very personal to the global" ("Introduction," p. xxviii). Based in Uttar Pradesh in India, Sangtin Yatra critically interrogated "the manner in which social hierarchies based on caste, class, religion, and geographical location become central to understanding the interrelationship among women's empowerment, NGO work, and the politics of knowledge production" (ibid., p. xxiii) while intentionally blurring the boundaries between creative, academic, and other forms of writing across genres and languages.

Connolly-Shaffer (2012) also addresses collective praxis, focusing on the transformative and healing potential of sharing feminist testimonies through polyvocal sharing in *Staging Cross-Border (Reading) Alliances: Feminist Polyvocal Testimonials at Work*. She asserts that testimonies brought into dialogue pave the path for the narration of the truths that create new social knowledge. Connolly-Shaffer elaborates:

> By undercutting the notion that any single narrated experience can provide an objective, unmediated, version of "Truth," polyvocal testimonios embody a theory of partial perspective, insisting that while our lived subject position necessarily informs what and how we know, our experiential knowledge must be brought into dialogue with others in order for it to mean beyond ourselves. By interlinking individual women's life stories, and positioning these truths alongside each other in the narrative frame, polyvocal feminist testimonios structurally allow for a larger, collective "Truth" to cautiously emerge, and thus conceptually and narratively realize the significance of this sentiment. (p. 144)

In that sense, the polyvocal feminist testimonios can transform from the individually situated experience into a claim of and creation of social knowledge only when brought together in a dialogue.

All three examples of collective memory work have instigated important methodological and ethical directions for the situated praxis of collective memory writing with the young refugees foundational to solidarity movement building. Drawing on Haug (1999), the process of collective writing of memories with young refugees was a learning one, as we have experienced coming together and closer to each other in the mutual process of learning, unlearning and relearning—with the blurring of boundaries between the researcher and researched. Drawing on Nagar (2006), collective memory writing indeed was a process of articulating and sharpening a critique of social injustice and systems of power. Drawing on Connolly-Shaffer (2012), the collective work with refugee youth has yielded the production of social knowledge critical to political claims and the social movement in the making. The collaborative process of writing and the emergence of collectivity was and has been an experience of transformation and healing that unfolded by unearthing the silenced, subjugated, and erased truths (Bang, 2016; Nagar, 2006; Shafak, 2020).

Weaving in critical pieces

The collective memory writing session with six of seven young refugees took place in the nearby village of Belišće, a town only a few kilometers from the Croatian-Hungarian and Croatian-Serbian borders; both borders are sites of well-established border protection regimes and police violence against refugees. My earliest experiences facilitating working sessions, which demand high personal investment due to the emotional and intellectual labor necessary to provide rigorous social critique, taught me about the importance of location, space, and time. The location wherein the collective memory writing session took place was close enough to a nearby border, whose disturbing presence centered our memory writing and enabled us to undertake a deep dive into the border politics and governmentality's wrongs. At the same time, it was far enough away that the space we used for the labors of writing, sharing, scrutiny of wrongs, cooking, and resting was a safe one. Our sanctuary for four days was the *Citadela Farm*, led by the community organization Zvono (*Bell*), which develops inclusive landscapes for children and youth with disabilities. We were hosted in two wooden houses with an outdoor space that we used for writing and our discussions. It was located deep in the forest, and for three mornings in a row we would wake up to the sound of birds and drink our morning tea with a cheerful bunch of local youths who took care of the land and Zvono's garden. On hot days, our hosts would evacuate the farm around 10 in the morning and leave seven of us in the shade of tall trees in the oldest European oak forest to focus on our memory work. Our days were paced in these landscapes that kept inviting our creative energies and connection with *self* and the *collective*. Apart from the location and space, the time played a crucial role in allowing the labor of focused writing, lengthy conversations, and returns to lingering questions. The time enabled reminders of personal epistemes and agencies that have so often been overlooked, stolen, or dismissed as refugee youth shared in their narrations. The time allowed both research and writing to transition to activism and imagination of possibilities. The careful choice of location, space, and time, devoted to the intentional labor of disrupting epistemological and political frameworks of the current securitized migration and refugee regimes, was the first critical piece of the situated collective memory writing.

That hot morning in early July when we traveled to the *Citadela Farm* was the first time that any of us crossed the borders of the towns of Sisak and

Zagreb, the towns where we lived at the time. It was the first time that any of us had traveled during the COVID-19 pandemic, and the first time that refugee youth were on the move for a purpose that wasn't forced or part of the struggle for survival. We drove in two separate cars to the eastern part of the country, which was the area that first encountered *the long summer of migration* in 2015, with its mass arrivals of refugees and migrants from the SWANA region (Kasparek & Speer, 2015). We spent the early afternoon in informal conversations and indulgences in the food that Zvono's director, Mira, graciously prepared for our lunches each day. Learning about each other felt rewarding as we walked in the forest and the spacious garden areas, and as we encountered wildlife. Our first outbursts of laughter occurred with the fear of flies and bees buzzing around and unknown creatures crawling about. However, the first feelings of unease and memory occupied our bodies as we ran into the MINE FIELD signage surrounding us. (The area has not been de-mined since the war in the former Yugoslavia at the beginning of the 1990s.). Our movements in the oak tree paradise were cautious.

We began our collective memory writing session at the large table by drawing our life paths on a piece of paper. After the prior experiences of narrative inquiry and collaborative autoethnographies, established relationships among some of us, and friendships that had blossomed on the earlier car ride, our novel and refreshing setting invited personal flows to emerge. We engaged in the activity "My life through time" by drawing attention to the critical junctures in our life journeys. With many fond life memories marking our journeys, each of us excavated *taboo memories* (Shohat, 2006) of war, refuge, childhood struggles, deportations, as well as the experiences of racialization, gendering, and cultural and epistemic erasures in schools. As each of these memories saw the light of the day, they were accompanied by sighs and words articulating how these were hard to tell, or even forbidden from being told. The unfolding of these layers resonated with Shohat's (2006) discussion on *taboo memories* explained as

> Memories that endanger the hegemonic narrative are forbidden, expelled, proscribed. Their marking as taboo ends up being internalized, even if only unconsciously, by the scarred bodies and souls who might have desired to tell history in a different way, from an alternative angle or perspective . . . taboos endemic to . . . single-ethnicity, single-nation, single-religion, or single-issue analytical framework. (2006, p. xix)

The revelation of seven personal accounts inhabited our time and shared space. This interlude in the labor of writing exposed the vulnerabilities of each of us sharing memories that represented life-long struggles. What emerged among us resonates with Nagar's (2019) *radical vulnerability* that "seeks to re-imagine the temporalities and meanings of knowledge-making partnerships by surrendering to a politics of co-traveling and co-authorship. . . . A relationality embedded in radical vulnerability strives to internalise that our self is intensely co-constituted and entangled with the other" (p. xx). Moreover, this interlude paved the way for acquiring a sense of collective belonging to a process with unfoldings yet to be seen. We never parted ways at the end of the day for individual processing and space. With the sound of loud music and creative exchange of recipes, we occupied the tiny kitchen space, cooked a few dishes popular in Syria, and enjoyed dinner until the late hours.

As we flowed into a fresh conversation with the roosters' wake-up call, we moved with a different sense of community and relationality.

> "Being not the only one who suffered from being a refugee. It is good to know other's experiences."
>
> "You can feel that your story is not the only one that is difficult."
>
> "We learned that your story is not your own. There are more stories about refugee lives."
>
> "It is good to know that you are not alone in this."
>
> "It is also hard to learn about all the sufferings."
>
> "When we listen to other people's stories, we can relate. We can then see that they have experienced what you have experienced. Then they can talk about that afterward."

These were some of the meditations I quickly noted in my field notes. All of them speak strongly to the heartbreaking isolation that these refugee youth were pushed to. However, they also speak to the strong sense of relationality that was critical to collective memory writing and the notion of *collectivity* that would emerge during the rest of our encounter.

As my co-writers rounded up their impressions of our first day, I explained that the intention to fathom relationalities lured me to organize the collective memory writing work. The inspiring labor of transnational and decolonial feminists, as well as critical social movements, found relationality foundational to the praxis of solidarity that seeks political shifts. In that sense, memory writing and storytelling were the essence and instrument for living solidarities and movement building. This conversation, which unfolded around the notion of relationality and solidarity, along with the nodes of location, space, and time, was another critical thread in the collective memory writing piece.

Additionally, the labor of theorizing inevitably became part of the process. Haug (1999) explains that memory work has two espoused dimensions, one being collaboration and another being theorization and critical analysis of the discourse. Collective theorizing shifted theoretical discussions and political concepts from my dissertation and academic spaces to collective story sharing with youth who deployed their life experiences to conduct critical analysis while located in an oak forest surrounded by minefields and borders. Relatedly, Nagar (2006) elaborates on collaborative praxis as follows:

> Theory of collaboration is generated *as* praxis; that is, what matters in this intellectual and political journey is not just theory-as-product but also the activity of knowledge production, especially as a site for negotiating difference and power. Through process of negotiation and struggle within and beyond the collective, varied forms of knowledge evolving in specific places and institutions interact with one another to produce new forms of knowledge. (p. 154)

Drawing on Nagar, what became significant in the situated collective memory writing with SWANA refugee youth was the production of knowledge through theorizing and positioning refugee youth as political subjects asking "whether and how it can become a part of the [refugees'] individual and collective agency and serve the critical activism . . ." (p. 154).

Prior to the collective memory writing session, just as I was flowing out of the labor of documentation of seven single narratives with the ever-moving plates underneath, I approached my further research with an argument that refugee youth in Croatia are subjected to the forceful, perpetual, literal, and figurative displacements from everyday life, culture, and schooling in Croatia. Documented narratives showed strong ideological dislocations of these youth due to their racial, national, transnational, ethnic, gender, cultural, and other intersecting identities.

As we dove into the conversation about displacements caused by the wars, loss of homes, deportations, denial of protection, earthquakes, the COVID-19 pandemic, online schooling, and hegemonies of the Croatian language, we transitioned into a writing session centering on the theme and question: "Remember a time when you felt displaced, rejected, and unwanted in your schooling experience in Croatia. What were the words, acts, and context that made you feel displaced?" Naming a research question that is of concern to all participants and that "creates a sense of commonality" (Haug, 1999, p. 2) is another critical piece tied to collective memory writing. Naming a question in this situated example was the researcher's suggestion; however, it is after this exercise that the first emergence of *collectivity* and *us* will take place.

To deepen our analysis, I laid out a set of cards on the table, written in Arabic, Croatian, and English, that pictured the following items: Papers/Documents, Language, Veil, Center for Social Welfare, Deportation, Benefits, NGOs, Housing, Cafe, Beard, Friends, School, Bus, and Refugee Camp. The purpose of these cards was to instigate the collectively written accounts of schooling experiences. Each of the card titles was embodied in the stories, only to reveal that refugee youth encounter rejection every day in the places that should feel safe, nurturing, and empowering. On the contrary, their teachers, welfare and humanitarian workers, peers, neighbors, and bus drivers often take a proactive role in dislocating refugee youth from the cultural, socio-political, and economic spaces of Europeanness, whiteness, Christianity, and civilization, rendering them as racial and gendered Other. Relatedly, schools operate as *sites of suffering* (Dumas, 2014). My co-writers noted the following reactions:

"Why don't you leave my country and go to back to your own country?"

"I am feeling left out because I don't speak the language well enough."

"You can't join the swimming club because you are a refugee."

"You can't work here with that thing on your head."

"Take that veil off. You are in free Europe now."

"My teacher always greets me with 'Esselamu aleykum' because he thinks that all Syrians are Muslims."

The glimpse into the accounts of perpetual displacement of refugee youth drew us into the labor of unpacking labels and the politics of targeting Muslims, looking like Muslims, and migrants and refugees from Muslim countries. Lingering on these assertions, I introduced the concept of flattening Muslim identity, as well as the concept of *double foreignness* that intersects with *Muslimness* and *refugeeness*, both of which I wrote about extensively in my dissertation. My co-writers entrusted us with repeating parts of their individual stories that spoke to the multiple displacements based on their (non) Muslim identity and refugee experiences, all of which emerged in the times of intense anti-Muslim violence. Moreover, the concept of *multiple pandemics* strongly resonated with refugee youth who spotlighted Islamophobia and anti-Muslimness, control of migration and freedom of movement, xenophobia, racism, sexism, homophobia and queerophobia, militarization, patriarchy and abortion prohibition—the axis of violation of their transnational, national, ethnic, and religious identities, as well as their gender and sexuality. Here we experienced an eruption of *taboo memories* or even a revival of artifacts disclosing refugee epistemologies, including *queer refugee epistemologies* (Shakhsari, 2020). This living archive revealed critical epistemes about silences sitting under the pressures of the systems of oppression—refugee journeys, life in camps, perilous crossings of borders, new life amid a pandemic, exile from schooling and displacement by the earthquake, as well as fears, desires, sexualities, shames, and joys. Collective writing of our memories represented an experience of liberation of silenced truths of refugee epistemes and refusals to fit in with the racialized, religified, and gendered portrayals, and thus has represented a mode of political empowerment.

Immersions into political organizing occurred prior to the collective memory writing session for some of these youth. A few months into the narrative inquiry process, after getting to know Sondan, Reyhan, Aicha, and their families—especially after learning about their struggles, and due to reconnecting with fellow activists and cultural workers in Sisak—we jointly organized Women's Circle Sisak. Our initial encounter took place on the Iranian New Year *Norouz*, which fell on the first day of spring in 2021. We gathered in support of the global campaign *No Sanctions on Iran* while connecting with the transnational movement and local members with ties in Iran and the SWANA region affected by the long-imposed sanctions that impoverished lives and proliferated the politics of exile.

Also, prior to the memory writing encounter, after the recent resurgence of the Israeli occupation of Palestine and the killing of 28 children in May 2021, a group of feminist activists, including myself, organized the protest action *Reading for Palestine*. Aicha and Sondan decided to join activists, poets, journalists, and artists in reading poetry in memory of the murdered children, all in defiance of the ruthless occupation of Palestinian lives and land. Two courageous young women wrapped *kufiyah* around their necks, stepped onto the stage, took microphones, and read Mahmoud Darwish and Asmaa Azazieh's gut-wrenching poems in Arabic, causing many to break out in tears on a steamy afternoon at the Victims of Fascism Square in Zagreb. The two spoke, urging passion against oppression while standing in the fragility of their legal status and the risks of social rejection as women with hijab. They embodied *poetic justice* (Nagar, 2006), as other forms of justice were out of reach.

The energies of refusal, protest, and hope were carried to the collective memory writing session. As we reached the last day of our encounter, we came to the question: "*Where do we go from here?*" which alluded to the title of one of four masterpieces by award-winning filmmaker Nadine Labaki, whose female characters tirelessly seek ways to end inter-religious and inter-ethnic disputes and killings of men in a small Lebanese village with a long history of Muslim and Christian co-existence. One of our writers suggested creating a non-profit organization for Syrian youth living in Croatia; another agreed and suggested expanding membership to all refugee youth, especially those experiencing difficulties in schooling; yet another one recommended that the new organization should be a network, crossing the borders and reaching refugee youth in the Balkans, given that many young people are stuck at the border with no access to decent living conditions, let alone education. The heated conversation sparked many ideas and directions while resting on the language "we could," and "we should." We came to terms with the initiating of a network of young refugees living in Croatia, with an aim to improve their education experiences and lives.

Healing and imagination

A few co-writers shared that writing memories and stories was a place of healing. Sondan stated with emotion, "*I feel my soul again.*" While collective memory writing is not meant to be a therapy (Haug, 1999), it can indeed have a therapeutical and healing effect. All of the co-writers wanted to continue writing and organizing a movement for change. The conversation erupted in ideas of summer and winter camps, writing workshops, and sessions with all the other refugee youth who needed their souls to be healed.

Standing at the location of possibilities emerging in the current moment, I find the experience of collective memory writing to be a process that sharply articulated a critique of social injustice, unearthing the truths and perspectives structurally strained and taut in their Otherness. Freeing these knowledges from the vacuum of representations of the Muslim Other or the refugee Other integral to the *politics of miseration* (Shakhsari, 2020) relates to Hunt's poignant deliberation on the necessity of changing the representations of the Others in academic research because of "the quality of knowledge that comes from living alongside kin who remain invisible to my colleagues in the academy other than in representations of risk, subalternity, marginality and victimization" (Oza et al., 2020, p. 7). Moreover, the collective memory writing process was one of transforming the *self* into *collectivity*, reclaiming political subjectivities through knowledge production, yielding "new ways of being, valuing, and believing" (Lugones, 2010, p. 754). Even more so, collective memory writing became a critical site of the intentional construction of the collective identity, commitment, collaboration, decision-making, and representation, which is then more than a critique of injustice and instead a praxis and politics of hope and possibility-making.

The *how* of the collective and the collective memory writing journey came into being as the process, place, and time in which one's voice intentionally became a wheel of individual and collective knowledge production in solidarity. This intention requires everlasting attentiveness to sensibilities, wounds, fragilities, desires, strategies, struggles, and time for unraveling personal and collective intricacies to be shared intimately and publicly. Moreover, such endeavor rests on accepting the fragmented and always incomplete truths, facts, and memories (Connolly-Shaffer, 2012; Morrison, 1995), while nested in emotional labor and devotion to building trust.

The lasting effects of suffering, misrepresentation, and oppression often stand in the way of expressing our vulnerabilities as a means of trust-building; however, the calling to share vulnerability becomes central to shaping collectives as sites pursuing epistemic justice. Again, Nagar (2019) writes about the inevitability of *radical vulnerability* shaping critical movements when striving for social change by asserting that "the singular relearns to breathe and grow differently in the plural" while it "cannot be an individual pursuit; indeed, it is meaningless without collectivity" (p. 30). Thus, our collective memory process was an inception of harmonizing each person's breathing with the stream of the collective's breathing as we muddled through the memories, solidarities, and epistemic justice immersed in our vulnerabilities.

Years after initiating one of the well-known collective memory writing experiences with women in Berlin in the 1980s, Haug (1999) wrote, "In working with our memories, we are trying to do two things: to find out how we actively conform with existing power relationships; and also, where in the past there are 'sparks of hope' in which we recognise ourselves 'as the ones who are meant'" (p. 538). Relatedly, Toni Morrison (1995) poignantly writes that "the act of imagination is bound up with memory" (p. 98)

References

Bang, M. (2016). Towards an ethic of decolonial trans-ontologies in sociocultural theories of learning and development. In I. Esmonde & A.N. Booker (Eds.), *Power and Privilege in the Learning Sciences: Critical and Socio-cultural Theories of Learning*, 115–138. Taylor and Francis.

Beznec, B., & Kurnik, A. (2020). Old routes, new perspectives. A postcolonial reading of the Balkan route. *Movements: Journal for Critical Migration and Border Studies Regime*, *5*(1) https://movements-journal.org/issues/08.balkanroute/02.beznec,kurnik-old-routes-new-perspectives.html

Bužinkić, E., & Hameršak, M. (2018). *Formation and disintegration of the Balkan refugee corridor: Camps, routes and borders in the Croatian context.* Institute for Ethnology and Folklore Research, Centre for Peace Studies, Welcome Initiative and CEDIM—Centre for the Study of Ethnicity, Citizenship and Migration [Zagreb].

Connolly-Shaffer, P. K. (2012). *Staging cross-border (reading) alliances: Feminist polyvocal testimonials at work.* Doctoral dissertation, University of Minnesota. https://hdl.handle.net/11299/141437

De Genova, N. (2017). *The borders of Europe: Autonomy of migration, tactics of bordering.* Duke University Press.

Dumas, M. (2014). "Losing an arm": Schooling as a site of black suffering. *Race, Ethnicity and Education, 17*(1), 1–29.

GOOD Inicijativa 2020. (2020, May 19). *Zasto su neka djeca ostavljena na pristojnoj udaljenosti?* [Why are some children left at a decent distance?] http://goo.hr/zasto-su-neka-djeca-ostavljena-na-pristojnoj-udaljenosti/

Hamm, R. (2020). Editorial special issue: Collective memory work. *Other Education: The Journal of Education Alternatives, 9*(1), 4–6.

Haug, F. (1999). *Memory work: A research guide*. http://www.friggahaug.inkrit.de/

Haug, F. (2008). Memory work. *Australian Feminist Studies, 23*(58), 537–541.

Imagining Transnational Solidarities Research Circle (ITSRC) (2020). *Statement*. https://icgc.umn.edu/research/imagining-transnational-solidarities

Kasparek, B., & Speer, M. (2015): Of hope: Hungary and the long summer of migration. *Translation: Elena Buck*. Retrieved from: bordermonitoring.eu

Kuća ljudskih prava & GOOD Inicijativa. (2021, July 27). *Pravo na obrazovanje: Pregled stanja za 2020.* [The right to education: An overview of the situation for the year 2020]. http://goo.hr/pravo-na-obrazovanje-pregled-stanja-za-2020-godinu/

Lugones, M. (2010). Toward a decolonial feminism. *Hypatia, 25*(4), 742–759.

Nagar, R. (2019). *Hungry translations: Relearning the world through radical vulnerability*. University of Illinois Press.

Nagar, R.. (2015). *Muddying the waters: Coauthoring feminisms across scholarship and activism*. University of Illinois Press.

Nagar, R., & Sangtin Writers Collective. (2006). *Playing with fire: Feminist thought and activism through seven lives in India*. University of Minnesota Press.

Morrison, T. (1995). The site of memory. In W. Zinsser (Ed.), *Inventing the truth: The art and craft of memoir*, pp. 83–102. Houghton Mifflin.

Oza, R., Hunt, S., Minelle, M., & Misri, D. (2020, August 25). Book Review Symposium—*Hungry translations: Relearning the world through radical vulnerability*. Symposium. https://antipodeonline.org/2020/08/25/hungry-translations/

Shafak, E. (2020). *How to stay sane in an age of division*. Wellcome Collection.

Shakhsari, S. (2020). Displacing queer refugee epistemologies: Dreams of trespass, queer kinship, and politics of miseration. *Arab Studies Journal, 28*(2), 108–133.

Shohat, E. (2006). *Taboo memories, diasporic voices*. Duke University Press.

Zia, A. (2019). *Resisting disappearance: Military occupation & women's activism in Kashmir*. University of Washington Press.

About the Authors

Karla E. Atoche-Rodríguez is a Doctoral Candidate at the Universidad de País Vasco (Spain). She has a Bachelor's in Education and a Master's Degree in Human Ecology. Her research interests are in evaluation, environmental education, teacher and administrator professional development. Currently, she is working as an evaluator for the Centro de Evaluación Educativa de la Secretaria del Gobierno del Estado de Yucatán, Mexico. E-mail: karla.atoche@yucatan.gob.mx

Emina Bužinkić is an activist, scholar, and writer from the Balkans laboring at the intersections of migration, education, and globalization. She engages with anti-militaristic, anti-capitalist, and anti-racist political praxes. Her work is inspired by migrants' everyday struggle for freedom and epistemes emerging from transnational and feminism, critical border activism, and collective knowledge production. She is a member of AGITATE! Unsettling Knowledges Editorial Collective, Transbalkan Solidarity, and Transbalkan Tribunal for Justice.

Jill Channing, Ph.D. serves as assistant professor and department chair for the Department of Educational Leadership and Policy Analysis at East Tennessee State University. She has published on a variety of topics related to higher education teaching, leadership, and cultural studies.

Edith J. Cisneros-Cohernour obtained her Ph.D. from the University of Illinois at Urbana-Champaign (UIUC). Her research focuses on improving educational quality, especially in the evaluation and development of academic staff, school organizations, and program evaluation, as well as the study of ethical and equity issues in research and evaluation. She is a member of the National System of Researchers (SNI-II). Dr. Cisneros has published her research in prestigious journals in Latin America, the United States and Europe.

Anita Franceschi holds a Bachelor's Degree in Social and Organizational Psychology and a Master's Degree in Clinical Dynamic Psychology. After a year of research in the area of social dangerousness and the restraint of offenders diagnosed with mental illness, she currently works in the field of social and economic marginality to promote inclusion and the creation of solidarity networks.

Roger J. González-González has a PhD in Social Sciences. He is the author of various articles, book chapters, books and presentations at academic events. He has teaching experience at the undergraduate and postgraduate levels in institutions such as UADY and the National Pedagogical University. His research areas focus on social and educational justice, youth participation in higher education, science and technology, as well as the evaluation of educational programs and policies. He is a member of the CONACYT National System of Researchers.

Ezequiel Korin is an Assistant Professor of Spanish-language Media at the University of Nevada, Reno. His research explores the relation of digital technologies and societies from the theoretical approach of critical and cultural studies.

Monica Massari is Associate Professor at the University of Milan where she teaches Sociology of Memory, Comparative Social Systems and Global Societies and Rights. Since the early 2000s, she has been focusing on Mediterranean migration with a special focus on gender dynamics, the process of social construction of otherness and new forms of racism in Europe. Currently her research interests focus on the study of traumatic memories related to migration with a growing attention toward the use of biographical methods and narrative approaches.

Aravindhan Natarajan's professional interests involve the use of the Arts in Social Work Practice and Research. He uses photography, painting, sketching and other art forms to explore issues of social and economic justice. He has incorporated his original Art in Autoethnographic narratives and performances. His Arts-Based Evocative Autoethnography, 'Art-Making in Public: Impacting Positive Transformation,' was published in 'New Directions in Theorizing Qualitative Research – Performance as Resistance' (Edited by N. K. Denzin & J. Salvo).

Cathy Raymond has a doctoral degree in Literacy, Culture, and Language Education from Indiana University, Bloomington. She has a passion for collaborative interdisciplinary research in cross-cultural studies, teacher education, and narrative studies. Her research is guided by social justice principles, with a focus on educational equity, culturally and linguistically responsive teaching, plurilingualism, and the amplification of participants' lived experiences. She is currently writing a nonfiction book with her Afghan research partner.

Carol Rogers-Shaw, Ph. D., is an adjunct professor at the University of Dayton. She earned a doctorate in Lifelong Learning and Adult Education from Pennsylvania State University. She is the co-editor of Adult Learning, an international, peer reviewed, adult education practice-oriented journal. Dr. Rogers-Shaw's research focuses on expanding educational inclusion for disabled adults, stigma and disability disclosure, transition to postsecondary education, graduate study, profound learning, and Universal Design for Learning.

James Salvo is the associate editor of three journals. He and Jasmine Ulmer co-edit series pertaining to research methodologies and host a podcast (researcherscardbox.com).

Ciro De Vincenzo is a clinical and community psychologist. He has a PhD in Social Sciences, and he lectures on "Community Psychology" and "The Psychology of Social Phenomena" at the University of Padova. He works at the intersection of border, trauma, memory, and migration studies from a socio-cultural and political psychological perspective. He is interested in understanding how marginalized communities or groups react to different types of violence and how they trigger societal transformation.

Georgina E. Wilson, Ph.D., spent 20 years as a public school educator working to mitigate the effects of environmental and educational barriers for students, including creating a trauma-informed program model to meet students' social emotional needs, with the use of mindfulness and restorative practices. She is currently an assistant professor of educational leadership at Central Michigan University. In that position, she helps prepare current and future school administrators serving as faculty and program director.

Index

A
Adams, T., 41
Adichie, C., 120
Ajuwon, A., 56
Al Jazeera, 125
Alexander, B., 60
Alexander, J.C., 41
Alexander, M.J., 118, 121
Allen, M., 103
Amadasun, S., 18
analytic autoethnography, 104
analytical memos, 126
Anderson, B., 46
Anderson, L., 104
Anderson, R.C., 23
Arnett, R., 59
art-based narratives, COVID lockdown and, 75–77, 77–81, 81–82, 82–85, 85–87, 87–89, 89–92, 92–96
  camping to socialize, 85–87
  Cleveland Orchestra and, 75, 76, 94
  food shopping, 77
  getting vaccinated, 89–93
  home life, 77–81
  quality time with family, 93–96
  remote teaching, 81–82
  venturing out, 83–85
  writing, 87–88
ATLAS.ti, 27
autoethnography, 102–3, 103–4
  analytic, 104
  evocative, 103–4
  layered, 104
Azazieh, A., 145

B
Baglieri, S., 110
Balakrishnan, V., 55
Bang, M., 138
Bárcena, A., 8
Baumgarten, L., 102, 113
Bergmark, U., 26
Berkovich, I., 24, 25, 35
Berry, B., 24
Beznec, B., 135
Blevins, A., 23
Bochner, A.P., 87, 100, 102, 104
Bolander, B., 41
Bolter, D., 62
book chats, 128
Boss, P., 112
Brown, K.M., 25
Bruce, E.J., 112
Bryson, S.A., 35
Butler, S.E., 43
Bužinkić, E., 134

C
Caicedo, V., 18
Cambodia: A Book for People Who Find Television Too Slow, 105
Cambron-McCabe, N., 25
Capper, C.A., 25
care ethics, 26
caring climate, 29
caring spaces, 31
Carr-Chellman, D., 101
Casanova, J.A., 15
Chiseri-Strater, E., 126
Chowdury, E., 119
Citadela Farm, 139
Clandinin, D.J., 121
Clark, M.C., 102, 113
Cleveland Orchestra, 75, 76, 94
Cloud, D.L., 119
co-constructed interview conversations, 128
Cocorullo, A., 41
Colás-Bravo, P., 11
collaborative autoethnographies, 136
collaborative cross-cultural research, 128
collaborative research design, 118
collective, 139
collective analysis, 137
collective memory writing, refugee youth and, 133–36, 136–38, 139–45
  healing, imagination and, 145–47

collective praxis, 137
collective writing. *See* viral epistolary
collectivity, 141, 143, 146
commonality, sense of, 143
Community of Inquiry (CoI), 101
Connelly, F.M., 121
Connolly-Shaffer, P., 137–38, 146
Conroy, T.J., 34
Contreras, G., 16–17
Corbera, E., 24, 35
correspondence letters, 44
co-travelers, 136
COVID-19
  cases and deaths from, 9
  education, research and, 9–12, 18
  impact on society, 8–9
  researching disabilities during, 107–13
Coward, R., 65
Cowley, S.J., 59
Creswell, J.D., 26, 121
Creswell, J.W., 12, 26
critical ethnographic narrative inquiry, 134
critical feminist disability theory, 110
cross-border reading alliance, 137
cross-cultural feminist research, 117–19, 122–29, 129–130
  background of project using, 119–20
  narrative inquiry and, 120–21
  project overview, 120–22
Cupples, J., 57
cultural humility, 123, 124, 130

D
Danforth, S., 110
Darwish, M., 145
Das Argument Kolektiv, 137
Davis, C., 59
decolonizing research methods, 121
De Genova, N., 134
DeMartino, L., 23
Demertzis, N., 41, 46
Denzin, N.K., 19, 99
Dewey, J., 33
Digital Ethnography, 18
Disability Studies in Education (DSE), 110
dissertation, finishing during COVID, 99–100
  Community of Inquiry and, 101
  critical feminist disability theory and, 110
  peer support group and, 100–1
  researching disability and, 107–13
  split-page autoethnography format and, 102–3, 105–7
  writing about disability, 101–2, 106–7
Dodds, T., 59
Doecke, B., 121
Dogan, V., 60
Dominguez, R., 25
Donner, J., 59
Doore, S.A., 100
double foreignness, 144
Drouoin, M., 59
Dumas, M., 143
Durlak, J.A., 24
Dvoskin, N., 8

E
Eadie, P., 23
Economic Commission for Latin America and the Caribbean, 9
educational leadership educators, study of
  culture of caring and, 23–24, 35–36
  creation of caring spaces, 29–31
  description of participants in study, 27–28
  developing caring relationships and, 31–32
  implications of study for practice, 36–37
  implications of study for research, 36
  learning objectives, adapting and, 32–34
  literature review of, 25–26
  methodology of study, 26–27
  racial norms and, 25–26
  reflexive statements by participants, 28–29
  theoretical framework, 26
  wellness, mental health and, 34–35
Elias, M.J., 24, 101
Ellingson, L., 103
Ellis, C., 87, 99, 100, 102, 103, 104
emerging remote education (ERE), 17–18
empathy, 120
epistemic authority, 118, 121
epistemic violence, 118
Erll, A., 41
Escudero, X., 7
Etmanski, A., 110, 111
ethics of care, 32
Eveleigh, A., 24
Evocative Autoethnography, 87
evocative autoethnography, 103
Eyal, O., 24, 25, 35
Eyerman, R., 41, 46

F
Falcón, S.M., 121
Fawcett, B., 105, 107
fear of missing out (FoMO), 60
Ferri, B.A., 107
Fester, M.-T., 59
first-order coding, 27
flexibility, 124, 127, 130
Floyd, G., 81–82
Forty Rules of Love, The, 124
Fowler, C., 119
Frandsen, L.N., 41
Frauenformen, 137
Furman, G., 25

G
Gabel, S.L., 110
Gamiño, M., 16
Gan, C.L., 55
Gardner, S.K., 100
Garland-Thomson, R., 110
Garrison, D.R., 101
gendered orientalism, 119
Gerstl-Pepin, C., 24, 25, 35
Gilligan, C.J., 26
Goldberg, N., 88
Goldstein, L.S., 23
Gonzalo-Eslava, D., 10
GOOD Initiative, 133
Gorman, E., 112
Grusin, R., 62
Guba, E.G., 19

H
Haggis, J., 43
Häggström, F., 23
Hameršak, M., 134
Hamm, R., 137
Harrington, W., 63, 65
Harris, A., 41
Harris, D.L., 112
Haug, F., 137, 138, 142, 143, 145
Hawk, T.F., 24
hegemony, 107
Held, V., 23
Highfield, T., 59
Hine, C., 18
Holmes, M., 43
Honoring, 118, 121
Horstmanshof, L., 56
Hoyt, L.T., 23
Hrastinski, S., 56
Huppatz, K., 41
hypermediacy, 62

I
Imagining Transnational Solidarities Research Circle, 136
information and communication technologies (ICTs), 11
Inter-American Development bank, 7
International Congress of Qualitative Inquiry (ICQI), 87
intimate journalism, 63
intrusive messaging, 63, 68
Ivermectin, 89

J
Jacobs, A., 113
Johnson, M.C., 8
Johnston, O., 24
Jutarnji list, 135

K
Kabul University, 125, 127
Kasparek, B., 134, 140
Kennedy, C., 56
Kim, J.-H., 121
Kinshuk, K., 55
Kitayama, S., 60
Kopelman, S., 41
Kozinets, R., 18
Kuća ljudskih prava, 133
Kurnik, A., 135

L
Labaki, N., 145
Ladd, L.D., 112
Laestadius, L., 18
Lai, C.K., 120
Lathen, L., 18
layered autoethnography, 104
Learn at Home, 7
learning management system (LMS), 55, 56
Levy, M., 56
Lewis, J., 88
Lincoln, Y.S., 19
Lindgren, C.L., 112
line-by-line coding, 27
Ling, R.S., 59

Linton, M., 102
literacies of globality, 117
Liu, B.F., 23
long summer of migration, 134, 140
Lugones, M., 146
Luka, M.E., 41

M
MacDonald, K., 119
Maddrell, J.A., 101
Madrid Akpovo, S., 24
Madrigal, L., 23
Manguel, A., 63
Mannon, B., 121, 123, 130
Markham, A.N., 41
Markus, H.R., 60
Martínez Franzoni, J., 9
Masiero, M., 46
Matassi, M., 63
Matejčić, B., 135
Matthewman, S., 41
Maufroy, M., 124
McCarthy, M.M., 25
McClellan, R., 25
McDowell, S.D., 119
McKenzie, K.B., 25
Merriam, S.B., 102, 113
Mertova, P., 121
Meurant, R.C., 55
Mexican Council for Science and Technology, 15
Mexican Department of Education, 7
Mexican universities, teaching and learning during COVID, 7–8
  challenges to Mexican universities, 7
  qualitative projects at, 15–17
  student resistance to classroom teaching, 8
  students' reaction to qualitative research, 13–15
  teaching qualitative courses during COVID, 12–13
migrant crisis, 134
Mijangos, J.C., 19
Miltner, K.M., 59
Minoldo, S., 8
m-Learning solutions, 55
Mohanty, C.T., 118, 121
Morrison, T., 146, 147
Moustakas, C., 26
multiple pandemics, 144
Muslim Other, 146
Muslimness, 144
Mutua, K., 121

N
Nagar, R., 136, 137, 138, 141, 145, 146
Narayan, P., 75, 77
narrative inquiry, 120–21, 136, 137
National Institute of Statistics and Geography (INEG), 18
Ne'eman, A., 102, 109
Netnography, 18
new collective space, 117, 123, 128, 130
No Sanctions on Iran, 144
Noddings, N., 23, 29, 30, 31, 32, 33, 34
Norsworthy, K., 121
not knowing, 123

O
Olshansky, S., 112
Omashta, M., 126
online focus groups, 18
openness, 122, 123, 130
Ortíz, J.C., 16
other, 135
Othering, 118, 121
Otherness, 146
Oza, R., 146

P
Page, J., 23
Palma, Y., 17
Parakh Theatre, 137
participant-generated data, 128
Patrick-Ott, A., 112
Paulus, T., 27
Perry, M., 117, 123, 130
Persky, J., 35
Pickering, M., 46
Piepmeier, A., 110
Pignatelli, F., 34
Pimmer, C., 63, 68
Pink, S., 18
Pirandello, L., 71
Playing with Fire, 137
Plester, B., 58
Plummer, K., 43
poetic justice, 145
politics of miseration, 146
Polkinghorne, D.E., 121

polyvocal feminist testimonio, 137, 138
postcolonial feminist theory, 121
Poth, C., 121
preferences of communication, 30
Primdahl, N.L., 23
problem-based learning, 12
professional learning communities (PLCs), 37
project-oriented learning, 12
prompt letters, 44
Przybylski, A.K., 60

Q

qualitative research
  social context of, 18–19
  teaching-learning process of, 11, 12
queer refugee epistemologies, 144

R

Rabin, C., 24
radical vulnerability, 141, 146–47
Rambe, P., 63, 68
Ramírcz, N., 15–16
Rasul, A., 119
Raymond, C., 124
Reading for Palestine, 145
reflexive activism, 137
refugee crisis, 134
refugee Other, 146
refugeeness, 144
research training, 11
researcher-driven practice, 118
re-storied findings, 128
Rieman, D.J., 26
Rogers-Shaw, C., 100, 101, 102, 105, 106, 107, 108, 109, 110, 111, 112, 113
Ronai, C.R., 104, 106
roomies, 67
Rosen, L.D., 58
Rossiter, M., 102
Rumi's Daughter, 124

S

Saldaña, J., 126
Salinger, J.D., 60
Salmons, J., 18
Salvatore, S., 46
Samermit, P., 59
Sánchez Ancochea, D., 9
Sangtin Kisan Mazdoor Sangathan, 137
Sangtin Writers Collective, 137
SARS-CoV2. See COVID-19
Schultz, C., 112
Scornavacca, E., 56
second-order coding, 27
Segal, E.A., 120
self, 135, 139, 146
self-reflection, 123, 130
self-reflective memos, 126
Sen, A., 8
Shafak, E., 124, 138
Shakhsari, S., 144, 146
Shen, R., 55
Shohat, E., 140
sites of suffering, 143
Sivarajah, P., 75
škola na daljinu, 135
Sleeter, C., 25
Smith, P., 41
SMS (short message service) pedagogy, 55–60, 60–67, 67–70, 70–71
  intimacy with students, 58
  student disconnect and, 69
social and emotional learning (SEL), 24, 34
social empathy, 120
solidarity, praxis of, 142
Soncini, A., 24
Sorrells, C., 24
Southwest Asia and North Africa (SWANA), 134, 136, 142, 144
Speer, M., 134, 140
Spivak, G., 118
Staging Cross-Border (Reading) Alliances, 138
Stanley, L., 43
Stone Sunstein, B., 126
Swadener, B.B., 121

T

taboo memories, 140, 144
Tamboukou, M., 43
Tateo, L., 46
Taylor, S., 110
Terman, R., 119
testimonies, 138
text speak, 59
textisms, 58
Thakur, K., 18
Thompson, L., 57
Thorndahl, K.l., 41
Tolins, J., 59
trauma-informed pedagogy, 33

Tretiakov, A., 55
trust, cultivation of, 124, 130
Tuhiwai Smith, L., 121
Turkle, S., 58

U
UNICEF, 12
United Nations, 9–10, 18
United Nations 2030 Agenda, 11
(UN)safe identities, 134

V
Valente, J.M., 110
Valicenti-McDermott, M., 23
Varga, M.A., 27
Vedantam, S., 120
Victims of Fascism Square, 145
viral epistolary, case study of, 41–42, 47–50, 50–51
  case analysis of study, 43–45, 45–46
  methodology of study, 42–43
Virtual Ethnography, 18
virtual interviews, 18

W
Wagner-Pacifici, R., 46
Webster, L., 121
Weissberg, R.P., 24
Wild Mind—Living the Writer's Life, 88
Women's Circle Sisak, 144
Workgroup UnEqual, 133
World Bank, 8, 9
World Health Organization, 9

Y
Yang, C., 24
Yatra, S., 137

Z
Zapata-Garibay, R., 7
Zeiger, D., 119
Zia, A., 136
Zieher, A.K., 24
zoomies, 67
Zuluaga, L., 18
Zúñiga, L.M., 8
Zvono, 139